The Glory of Hoysala Queens

Belur Chennakeshava Temple

Rekha Rao

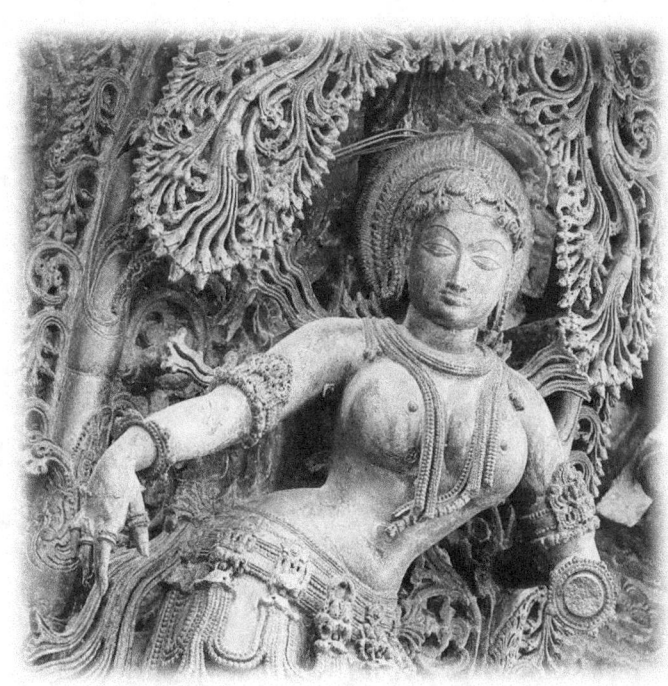

The Glory of Hoysala Queens

Belur Chennakeshava Temple

Year of Publication: 2019

ISBN: 9781075772245

Imprint: Independently published

Table of Contents

Intentionally Blank

The Glory of Hoysala Queens

Belur Chennakeshava Temple

1. Introduction

The enchanting bracket figures called Madanika or Shilabalika panels of Belur Chennakeshava temple are depicted like beautiful apsaras adorned with all jewellery and graceful postures. They have been a great source of inspiration for all the lovers of art. The female beauties projected as the celestial 'divyanganas' on a lotus pedestal are the classic and majestic examples of the art of Hoysla style and civilisation. They have successfully charmed the spectators ever since they adorned the walls of this temple. An insightful study of the ancient text Manasollasa compiled in 1126 A.D. and the activity depicting realism in the shilabalika figures, both belonging to the same period approximately revealed that they appear to reflect a social theme like about the lifestyle of queens of Hoysala dynasty. One of the Belur temple inscriptions records that Shantala, the queen of Hoysala king Vishnuvardhana was a great dancer and donated profusely for the support of artists. The other queens were also well versed in music, archery, games and so on. This book is devoted to the understanding of how the social life of queens of Hoysala dynasty was, based on the contemporary literary and archaeological documentations. The social, cultural and religious life in olden days revolved around the King and the queens. The progress and prosperity enjoyed by people depended on how efficiently the King engaged in promoting the welfare of his people. The social life of the royal families is also depicted in some of the panels adorning the temple walls.

The figures depicting social life have not been given as much importance as the study of sculptures of deities. An attempt has been made in this book to bring to light a neglected aspect of social life of queens of Hoysala period relating the 42 apsara sculptures of Belur with the description of queen's learning and hobbies as described in the ancient text Manasollasa. The bracket figures are numbered 1-42 in archaeological records starting from the first Figure on the right side at the entrance for historical documentations. The queen's depictions are according to the theme depicted and addressed as apsaras. These bracket numbers of archaeological records are not used in this book because the analysis is based on the text Manasollasa.

The concept of apsaras was a favourite theme in literary and architectural works of India. Their mention is seen in Rigveda 10.96.6, who were called water nymphs earlier and later ascended to firmament as friends of Urvashi and dancers of Indra's court. Apsaras in the archaeological representations of sculptural form are semi divines who destress and elevate the mind by their insight into art. As Shalabhanjikas (A lady holding the branch of shala tree) were seen as early as first century BC, in the gateways of Sanchi stupa. A continued tradition was represented in Hoysala period also who were depicted as beauties in the frame of flowery bush on an oval shaped lotus seat. The figures are addressed as apsaras in this book because of the concept and architectural placement above the earthly zone and queens were as beautiful and learned as apsaras. The attendant dwarf figures depicted in each apsara panel convey lot of information to understand activity of the main Figure. With this in focus, the analysis begins with who the main Figure relates to, who are her attendants and why she depicts multiple varieties of activities. The analysis is based on the study of Manasollasa and Natya shastra as main texts of reference.

2. Manasollasa as Textual Reference

Manasollasa is an ancient treatise, an encyclopaedic work in Sanskrit dealing with the political, social, cultural and religious aspects written by the Chalukyan king Someswara - III, in 1126-1138 A.D. He was the son of king Vikramaditya VI (1076-1126) who built the famous Mallikarjuna temple at Kuruvatti, Mahadeva temple at Ittagi, Kaitabheswara and Kalleswara temples. Manasasollasa is also called as "Abhilashitartha chintamani." Chintamani means a fabulous gem, that is supposed to yield its possessors all that is desired and Abhilashitartha is from the root word – Abhilasha – which means desired or longing for. King Someswara III was a noted historian, scholar and a poet. He authored the encyclopaedic work Manasollasa touching upon various topics like polity, governance, astronomy, astrology, rhetoric, medicine food, architecture, painting poetry, dance and music. He was titled Sarvajna bhupa and Bhulokamalla for his scholarly pursuit. Manasollasa is in Anushtub metre, with occasional prose passages.

Probably Chalukyan king Someswara intended to give any information sought about the Royal families, in his encyclopedia work. This exhaustive work is divided into five parts or Vimsatis, each further containing 20 chapters, totally presenting 100 chapters. Each chapter has a varying number of Slokas. The last and fifth part dealing with the amusements, sports, pastime hobbies of queens and social live of kings and queens is called "Raja Manasollasa".

The data documented in Manasollasa is in general a study of the life styles of the Chalukya, the Hoysala, the Kalachuris and the Yadava royal dynasties, who ruled the southern part of India during 1000 – 1400 A.D. The social life pattern is a progressive phenomenon evolving over a period. The information regarding the life styles can be viewed as that which existed in and around that period with the preceding and succeeding dynasties, and not restricted to the limited period of 1126 – 1138 A.D which was the compilation period of the text. All the 100 chapters throw light on the life of various sections of the society, with emphasis on royal families. The leisure and pleasure of royal women, their costumes, the fashion of the elite, their amusements and pastimes, are discussed in the 4th and 5th part of Manasollasa. The visual proof of this written document in Manasollasa can be seen in the female sculptures – Madanikas or apsaras in innumerable temples that were built during 11th, 12th, 13th and 14th centuries. In some temples these sculptures are coarse but in some they are exclusive and fine. But the apsaras of Belur Chennakeshava Temple are the ones, which exclusively depict the theme of social life of queens in the contemporary period of Manasollasa. The social aspects that are hidden in the apsaras sculptures, stand out, when observed keenly, keeping the 4th and 5th parts of Manasollasa as the background. There are many small figures depicting the everyday chorus of commoners in the lower bands of the temple outer walls. The apsaras stand out as individual figures with attendants and with different activities, which hint that the royal women enjoyed a high quality of upbringing, caliber, and hence they are placed high as bracket figures and categorized as apsaras popularly for they are like celestial beauties.

The Chalukyan and the Hoysala dynasties were very wealthy. The queens came from rich families, where the girls were groomed and learned in all branches of fine arts like music, dance, drama and literature. Women took part in debates and discussions and were well versed in adventurous sports activities also. The Chalukyan kings like the king Someswara III, in addition to their political prowess were also lovers of art, great musicologist, well versed in Natyasastra, Vishnudharmottara Purana and other texts related to music and knew the intricacies of the art of dancing and music. Natyashastra is the oldest surviving ancient Indian treatise of art of performance. The exact period of it is not known but the compilation is estimated to be between 500 B.C to 500A. D. The tradition attributes the authorship to Sage Bharata. Vishnudharmottara purana was an encyclopedic work compiled in 4th century A.D. Manasollasa is acclaimed as the text next to Vishnudharmottara purana which deals about the multiple aspects of political social, cultural life and household of Chalukya and Hoysala dynasties of Karnataka.

The Belur Chennakeshava temple was consecrated in 1117 A.D and the period of Someswara was 1126 A.D. A difference of 9 years can be viewed as a short period, when aspects of cultural and social heritage are considered. The literary data of Manasollasa text, and the archaeological proof of it can be considered as parallel thought process, emanating from two dynasties, as Hoysalas were initially feudators of Chalukyan rulers.

3. Approach

Belur is a small-town famous for the most beautiful Chennakeshava temple in Hassan district of Karnataka state. It is one of the best examples of Hoysala monuments and famous for the most beautiful Shilabalikas – the 42 apsara figures which are almost well preserved. The figures are 2.5 feet in height excluding the oval lotus pedestal and the canopy frame of a bush. These figures still reveal their devotional qualities, which existed during the height of Hoysala civilisation. With their hypnotic beauty, ever since they adorned this temple even after 900 years, these graceful dancing apsara still display their warmth and beauty. The scholarly poet Dr. D.V. Gundappa, mesmerized by the beauty of these sculptures has composed songs on each one of them and identified them based on the activity depicted with names like Darpana sundari, Shuka bhashini etc, which are very popular. Artists have been sculpting the replicas of these figures in all mediums like wood, stone, metal, papier-mâché etc and innumerable art historians and writers have given their imagination, based on the beauty and themes of these apsaras. Even to this day dancers are motivated to imitate the postures of these apsaras in their recitals.

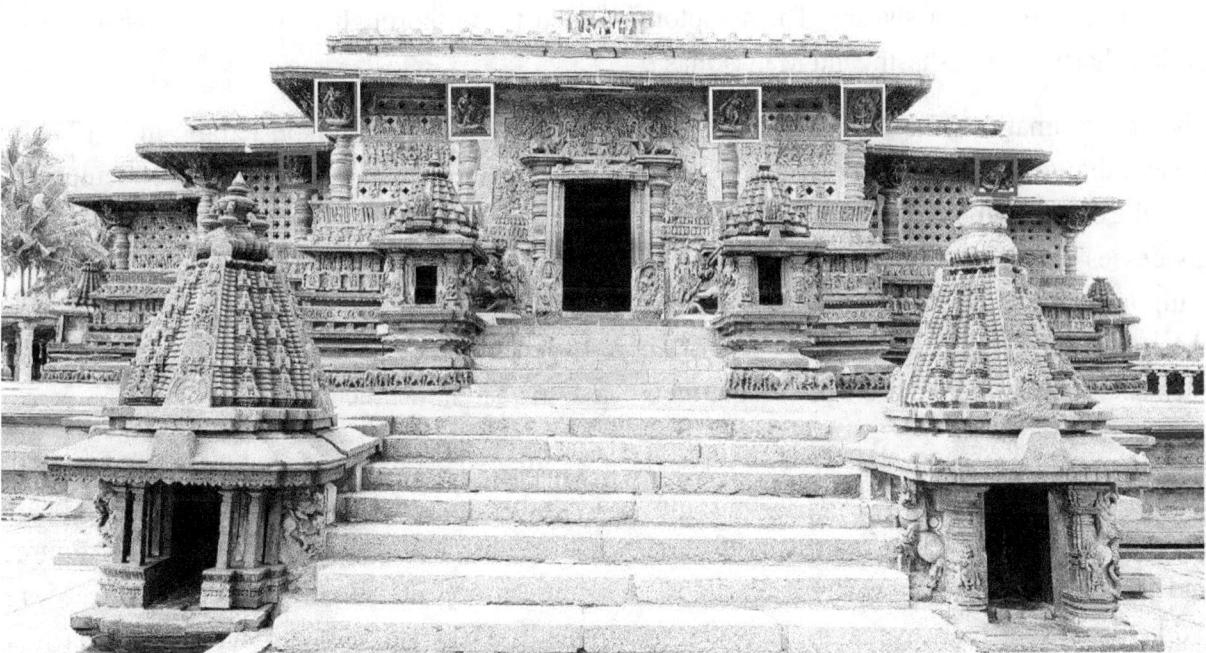

Figure 1: General view of Belur Chennakeshava temple with the Shilabalikas marked.

Born and brought up in a place called Mysore, this temple was the monument, which I frequented often on vacations, with the sole intention of understanding these apsaras figures that had caught my fancy. As a young girl undergoing training in Bharata Natya style of classical dance, I always wondered whether there exists a linkage between the present form of Bharata Natya and the apsara sculptures at Belur. I could notice that some looked like interpretative panels and some depicted pure dance movements. To me, they closely related to the personality of Nartaki, the main dancer as described in the Natyashastra.

The dwarf figures which are on either side of the apsara sculpture looked interesting to me for though they were depicted very short it looked very proportionate, dress code varied, and perform different roles. The dwarf figures were different for dancing figures and the figures of other activities like hunting or decorating themes. I could notice that they match with the description of the characters related to the assistants of the heroin or queen. "Duti Lakshana", a chapter (Part 2, 46) of the ancient text Dasharupaka by Dhananjaya, 10th century A.D, which is a commentary on some chapters of Natyashastra, describes the qualities and work portfolio of attendants of the heroin or the queen. To know more about these figures, I first classified the 42 apsara figures into recital and thematic based figures which gave some clarity of thought. But the figures were placed high on a pilaster connecting to the roof at an inclined angle like Bracket figures indicating about their status as higher than earthly.

In pursuit of this mission, I studied Indology at post-graduate level with specialization in Hoysala art and architecture. I could understand these 42 figures depicted resemble the description of a category of semi divines celestial dancers called apsaras or divyanganas who were positioned on lotus pedestal. Their body postures, leg and arm positions and accessories were according to the prescriptions of Natya shastra. The sculptors seemed to be thorough in their understanding of Shilpa shastra, Natyashastra and Manasollasa.

The apsara images were probably added after the completion of the main temple in 1117 AD. Hence, they obscure the original brackets. They also depict stylistic development of sculptures over the other sculptures of Belur temple. They bear closer resemblance to the images of Gods and goddesses around the upper walls of Halebid temple (1121 A.D- 1160 A.D) than the other sculptures at Belur. The Sculptors have not revealed anywhere about the scriptures of Shilpa shastra or the style and text of dance and music followed. But they have left their signatures under each sculpture, indicating self-praise and their pride, in accomplishments.

The lower bands of the wall in Belur temple also have many figures of dancing girls (see Fig. 2C). They are not given the lotus pedestal and show a different type of frame work of the plant. It bears a resemblance to the Chalukyan style of frame work (see Fig 2.A). The themes of bracket figures and the series of dancing figures are almost the same. It appears some figures or themes were worked out exclusively by the skilled leading sculptors like Jakkana, Mallitamma or chavana (their names are inscribed under each bracket Figure) at a slightly later period and fixed as bracket figures. The execution of bracket figures in Hoysala style (see 2.B) is very much refined, intricate and the quality of stone also looks better compared with the dancing figures on the lower band. The frame work of the bush is also different from that of dancers at the lower level in Belur. The attendants in bracket figures are more in number and dressed well too compared to the Chalukyan style. This gives a hint that the 42 figures were carved by the leading sculptors with a better understanding of the social life of queens as against the figures of dancers who were in service as paatra or the temple dancers.

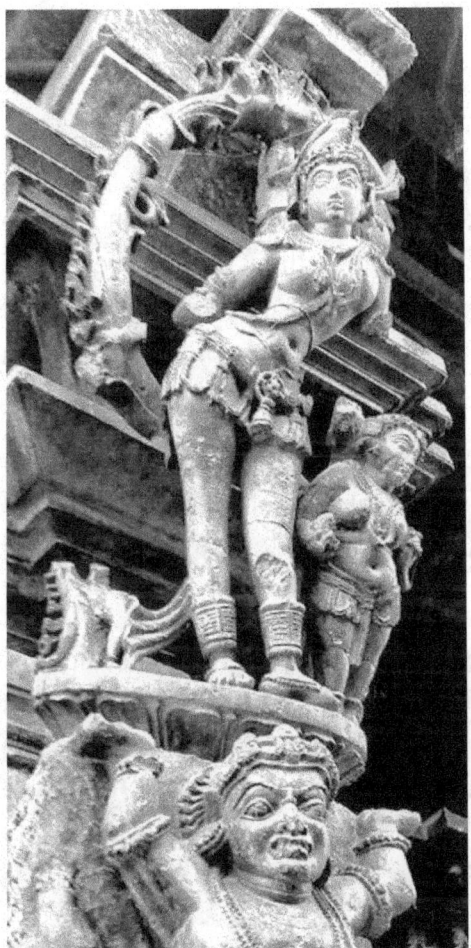

Figure 2A

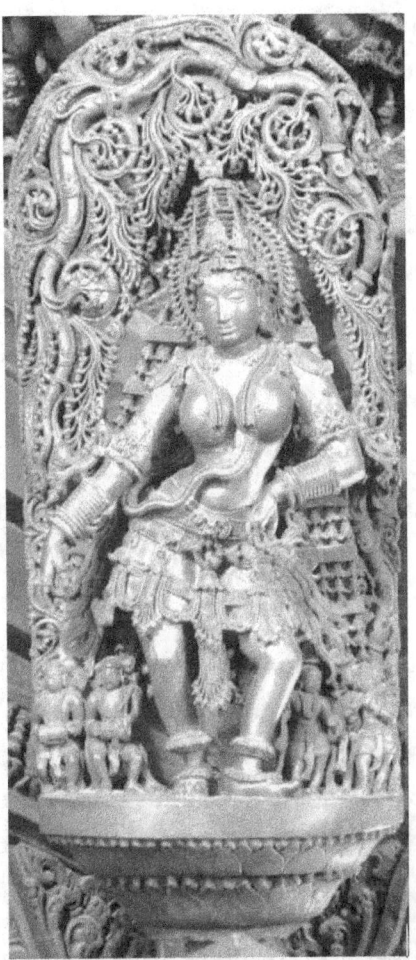

Figure 2B

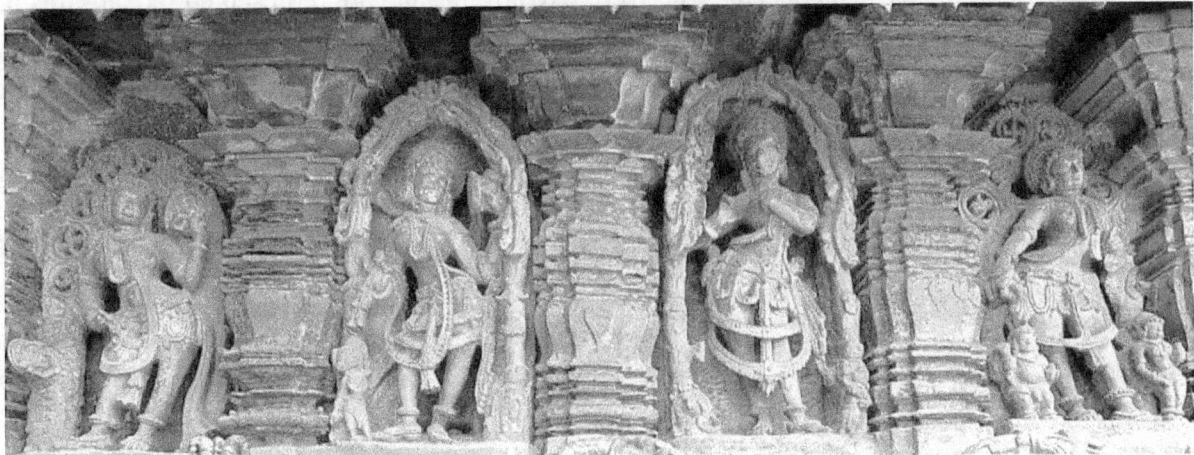

Figure 2C

Figure 2 A, B and C: A comparative account of apsara figures.

Figure 2A depicts the dancing Figure of Chalukyan style of Kuruvatti Mallikarjuna temple. Figure 2B of Hoysala style shows the refinements that were adopted in bracket figures. Figure 2C depicts the many figures of dancers on the outer wall of Belur temple at lower bands.

These apsaras, when viewed in the background of Manasollasa appears that queens of Chalukya and Hoysala dynasties were portrayed as role models to these sculptures displaying their status, skills, hobbies, and insight in the fine arts.

While understanding the social and cultural life of Chalukyas the book Manasollasa (compiled in 1100 A.D approximately) gave a clarity in understanding that these 42 apsara sculptures also correlated with the personality of the royal queens, their hobbies and pastimes as described in the last and fifth chapter. I could connect that the figures are the representation of queens but depicted in dance postures as prescribed in Natyashastra because the queens and kings were well versed in the art of dance and music.

Apsaras when viewed based on Natyasastra, highlights their dance postures. The expression of moods – the Navarasas / sentiments are detailed perfectly in these sculptures. Most of the elements of the Natyasastra categories like abhinaya, body postures, accessories costumes, jewelry, attendants, musical instruments, etc. are all seen in these 42 figures.

When viewed from the philosophical perspective of getting into the inner world, the sculptures also depict various stages of mind through "Gunas" such as Sattvik, rajasik and tamasic as described in Bhagavadgita. To me, they appeared to be the amalgamation of all three aspects. The wholistic perspective of sculptures are to be studied from three texts for what they signify by their outer looks, their perfect dance postures and the flow of philosophical perspectives hidden within the sculptures.

This book is focused only on the initial visual aspect of who they are and analyze their activities according to how it is described in Manasollasa. The research is devoted for a deeper understanding of the versatility of the Hoysala queens, who were like apsaras and are represented like apsaras in stone medium. The queens also served as temple dancer in service of God prior to their marriage who were socially addressed as Paatra – the main dance artist. Hence, both terms paatra and apsara are used in the analysis of the panels. A brief account of the historical data, why the medieval period witnessed a profusion of temple construction and why sculptures were depicted in a dancing posture are provided for general information.

4. Historical and Socio-Religious Aspects

Apsara figures in Belur temple look a bit plump, short and robust, with heavy breasts and a very small waist, which appears a bit unnatural in body proportions. The sculptors have adhered to the measurement of body parts, according to Shilpa shastra and Manasollasa also describe the royal and beautiful women to have slender waist with plump breasts and hips. Indian art must be judged from the standpoint of its motive, to grasp soul of the art and appreciate the hidden worth. The causes, that had affected the iconoclastic art, were the hard and fast rules laid down in the liturgical texts of medieval period the Agamas, in making the images, which were based on the idealized form of feminine beauty, and grace. The sculptors were not free to disregard these rules, and thus their imaginary skills took a second place.

It is interesting to know why and how the Chalukyan and the Hoysala dynasties could build so many temples and embellish them with intricate carvings. The historical, political, economic, social and religious conditions were conducive for the development of art and architecture. The late Chalukyas of Kalyana who ousted the Rastrakutas in 973 A.D. built many temples noted for their fusion of both northern and southern styles, as well as richness of sculptural details on walls and doorframes.

Chalukyas were succeeded by the Hoysalas who were in power for more than 300 years from 1022 AD to 1310 AD. This was the golden age of cultural activity, when the rulers patronized not only construction of over a hundred temples, but also other fine arts such as dance and music. Later, Hoysalas expanded the territory and ruled over the fertile basin between Tungabhadra and Kaveri rivers and built innumerable temples, big and small, in almost every village. Among them the most noteworthy temples are the Chennakeshava temple at Belur, Keshava temple at Somnathpura, Hoysaleswara temple at Halebid. The Chalukyan temples no doubt were the models for Hoysalas both in conception and design, but the art got polished in the Hoysala era. Other contributing factors for the fineness, delicacy and exuberance of sculptures in the Hoysala temples are:

- Technological advancement
- Dynastic greatness and
- Religious and social developments

Technological advancement: The primary technical advantage enjoyed by the Hoysala artists lay in cutting and transporting of rock. It became possible for them to build temples larger, more ornate and more often. The early Chalukyas, who used coarse-grained sand stone as medium for temple construction had their own limitations. Late Chalukyas and Hoysalas brought into usage chlorotic schist - a greenish or blue-black soap stone, which was softer than sand stone. The soapstone of volcanic origin, quarried in the neighbourhood, was soft when first dug and hardened on exposure to atmosphere. As this change of material was easier to carve and polish, it resulted in a revolutionary change in the sculptural art of Hoysala period.

The single cell (garbhagriha) became multicell, each cell with a vestibule leading to a large and common pillared hall. The pillars were lathe turned, profusely ornate, highly polished and each of them had a different design. The square ground plan, modified later into a simple star plan, further got developed, with the angular displacements to sixteen and more points. The more the number of angular offsets, meant more space for embellishment, which made the Hoysala temple look like a jewel box full of intricate carvings. The Chalukyan shrine motif of niche and solitary sculptures, was replaced by bands of figures, and sculptures, which were protected by the huge projecting and curved eaves running all through the exterior wall of the temple there by separating the Shikhara or the tower from the vimana walls.

The tower or shikhara also observed the stellate plan formed by a series of closely set horizontal tiers, rising one above the other and each tier decorated by a grouping of miniature shrines. The height of the shikhara thus became dwarfed. It was topped by a lower parasol shaped finial, the cupola. The temple stood on a spacious platform called Jagati, which followed the stellate body of the temple. It provided a spacious pradakshina patha - an open circumambulatory passage to view the ornamental facade at proximity. With these technological advancements in the total anatomy of temple parts, the Hoysala temples got a unique identity.

Dynastic greatness: Hoysala king Vishnuvardhana, known for his military enterprise and patronage for art, religion and culture was one of the most illustrious kings of Karnataka, ruled between 1108 to 1142 A.D. Hoysala architecture reached its zenith during his time. His ambitions were to release some province from Chola kings and put an end to the subordination of Hoysalas to Kalyani Chalukyas. His efforts are documented in the Belur Inscription of 1117 A.D.

The Hoysala dynasty rulers felt the need to demonstrate their own greatness and royal status by overshadowing the temples of the past, whether it was starting a new temple or adding to what was already built. The more wealth a dynasty had for its building projects the more powerful it appeared. The new land, which they acquired by conquest, was highly fertile with major rivers - Tungabhadra, Kaveri & Krishna and helped production of abundant agricultural outputs. This gave them an access to trade and market their produce, resulting in vast financial reserves. Hoysala Kings Vishnuvardhana and Vira Ballala II, were keen to promote themselves as ideal kings. Many inscriptions describe in idyllic terms, the abundant wealth and wellbeing of the people in the kingdom. This prosperity was used to build innumerable temples and maintain the vast number of artists and other staff who were in the service of God. Hoysala kings believed in the ideal thought of Matsya purana that, one who rejoices in making temples, gets everlasting riches and he is worshipped in heaven. This concept motivated not only the king, but the generals, ministers, merchants and commoners to extend outstanding support to temple building and public utility work like tank or mutt constructions. The idea which the king cherished born out of deep devotion to God, that- the excess wealth should be used solely for the religious institutions, got deep rooted in the minds of his subjects. Temples and tanks were built in the major cities, in trade routes, and

14

banks of rivers, which attracted many devotees. The lavishness of labour and the elaboration of detail of the Hoysala temple pattern attracted the skilled sculptors. The master sculptors and artists from other places got attracted to the material gains and considered it a prestige to work for Hoysala kings and ministers. The Hoysala architects used the emblem of a young man slaying the tiger as the motif to give a separate dynastic identity, which was positioned on the entrance door of the temple. The Hoysala Kings believed in the power of knowledge. The lion signified a beast, a demon or darkness. Under the threat of a lion, the courageous king drew the sword of knowledge and protected himself (and the people) from illusion of 'maaya' with the help of a shield, signifying dispassion.

Religious and social developments: Bittideva was the original name of Vishnuvardhana. He relinquished Jainism and embraced Sri Vaishnavism under the influence of Ramanujacharya and built number of temples in both phases. The active Bhakti movement in conjunction with the royal patronage resulted in vast temple building campaign. Hoysala rulers emphasized on oneness of God and practiced religious tolerance, which was meticulously followed by commoners. King Vishnuvardhana was a Vaishnavite, his elder brother Ballala I, was a devout Shaivite and his queen Shantala was a Jain devout. The broad-minded patrons promoted all sects with equal support. King Vishnuvardhana further emphasized his unbiased outlook by carving Shaivite sculptures on the walls of Vaishnavite temple or vice versa and Basadi was erected in the campus of a temple.

The Kalyana Calukyas promoted the values of donations for a religious cause through religious discourses exemplified by puranic stories. People were influenced and inspired to donate their wealth for the construction and maintenance of a temple. There are many inscriptions in temples dating back to 11th and 12th centuries, which give an account of the donations made for temples. The discourses that were conducted in temple premises were sometimes audio-visual in nature, which brought about an awareness of the moral values among people. The new awareness resulted in a prolific construction of temples and Basadis dedicated to immortalizing the names of loved ones like teacher, father, mother, husband, wife and so on. Hoysala rulers maintained this order, which was laid out by their Chalukyan overlords. Belur temple inscription states that huge donations were given by the queen Shantaladevi and other rich people, towards the maintenance of temple or construction of a Basadi. Temples were also centers where annual festivals like Sankranti (harvest season rituals) Ugadi (new year), Navaratri-the nine-ten days Dasara celebration, Deepavali (festival of lights) were celebrated. Large gatherings were fed, and images of Gods were taken on a procession called utsava. With bigger temples, the responsibilities also increased. Every temple had a caretaker called Sthanapati, who looked after the maintenance of the temple, its finance, and the priest, who performed the worshipping rituals.

5. The Adoption of Dance and Music in Temple Sculptures

A fact that intrigues the tourists and devotees while studying a medieval temple is, why the temples were studded with so many dancing sculptures. Sage Bharata (the compiler of Natyashastra) answers that dance is occasioned by no specific need. Dance has come to use simply because it creates beauty, grace, enthusiasm and attraction when performed. Dance is naturally loved almost by all people. It is eulogized as being auspicious and a source of amusement on the occasions like general festivity, attainment of prosperity, marriage, childbirth and so on. Dance adds grace, attraction, and enthusiasm to an occasion making it more interesting. From a philosophical view, dance is an expression of joy. It is the sway and harmony of mind and body in response to the nature of melodious, rhythmic or musical vibrations. It sets both the performer and the onlooker, into a movement of spirituality. Hence, dance is a sacred art for which reason Hindu Gods are represented in dancing postures-all having certain meaning and philosophy

Hoysala monuments involved lavish labor and skilled workmanship. To attract commoners to visit a temple, Hoysala rulers and architects believed more in the sculptural richness than architectural massiveness. In the medieval period, temples that were built between 9th and 13th Century AD across India, the noticeable feature was the inclusion of dancing sculptures in the form of apsaras on the outer walls or in the Navaranga. The Hindu temples and the Jain Basadis, whether built in Naagara or Vesara style (north and South) – depicted all deities in different postures. Special attraction was the dancing beauties in stone, as seen in the medieval period Konark temple, Khajuraho temples, and the Hoysala temples.

The question arises why even the social themes of queen's life projected in Belur temple are in dancing postures. The answer to this query is that the creators of both Manasollasa and the Belur temple, were all well versed in the Natyashastra, and knew the intricacies of dance and music. Sculptures were used as a media to express the thought process, be it in the field of fine arts or in the field of philosophy. Natyashastra got amalgamated with iconography and Shilpa shastra used it as a "sutra"- a base or foundation, on which sculptures of social, mythological and philosophical aspects manifested as structure.

The result of the influence of Natyashastra is reflected in the projection Hindu Gods, mythological personalities and the apsaras- all represented in dancing modes.

Even the social theme of a queen's enthusiasm in archery, or her joyous moments with her pets are depicted in a dance mode in stone meticulously observing the leg, hand and head positions, costumes and accessories that can be used as laid out in Natyashastra and in Manasollasa.

High literary activity and adoption of music and dance as forms of worship in temples were probably the reasons why dancing sculptures became an integral part of temple architecture. Various commentaries on the art of dance and dramaturgy were written between the 9th and 13th Centuries by poets and scholars. To mention a few, Dasharupaka by Dhananjaya (10th cen A.D),

Naataka Lakshana Ratnakosha by Saagaranandi were written between 920 - 1100 AD. Na tya Darpana was written by two Jain poets, Gunachandra and Ramachandra between 1100-1175 AD. The great poet Sharadatanaya in 12th Century AD, wrote a text Bhaava Prakaasika and Sangitarathakara was compiled by Sarangadeva. All these texts dealt in detail about the chapter the expressive part of dance and drama and music called Rasa and Bhaava. The rulers who were patrons of art were inspired by these texts and adopted them in their art and culture. Thus, the art of dance gained popularity and got channelized according to these texts as sutra for sculptures of temple construction.

To quote the words of Dr. S.R.Rao in the foreword note on the book "Apsaras in Hoysala Art - A New Dimension" by Rekha Rao,2009

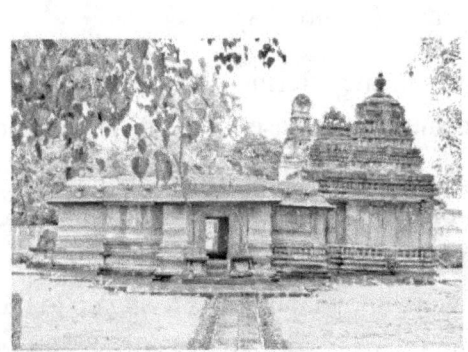

Figure 3A

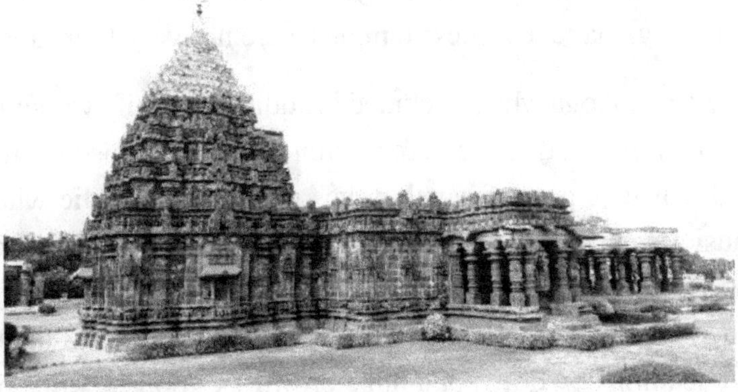

Figure 3B

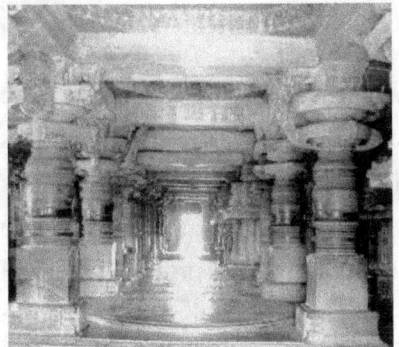

Figure 3C

Figure 3 A-C: Structure of Temples. Figure 3A: Angabhoga type, Kudali Rameshwara temple, Hoysala period. Figure 3B: Rangabhoga type, the structure of Ittagi Mahadeva temple of 12th century. Figure 3C: Hoysala Rangabhoga temple with a dancing platform in the pillared hall.

"Karnataka has a long tradition of royal patronage for art and literature and shared the common heritage of monumental culture of the Indian subcontinent. According to Kaavyamimaamsa of Raajasekhara, the King was himself expected to be a poet, artist, not for parading his intellect or aesthetic qualities, but for adjudging the literary equipment and artistic skill of his subjects and the need for preserving and enriching the monumental culture of the Kingdom. He should convene the assembly of poets and artists as was done by Bhulokamalla, Someshvara (1126-38 A.D.) the Kalyani Chalukyan king who refers to the Sabha or assembly of lovers of art in his famous work Abhilashitaartha Chintaamani or Raaja Maanasollasa."

As per the Hindu beliefs and inscriptional evidences, God is Live, and He is to be revered with different types of rituals and offerings. The same reverence was extended to the King, as he represented God on earth as Naradevata. The worship rituals that were offered to God were also extended to Kings. The temples evolved into two types namely angabhoga and rangabhoga. Angabhoga was a service rendered to the main deity, which included bathing, change of cloth, change of the sacred thread, application of sandal paste, lighting oil lamps and offering food as a token of respect and adoration to the deity embodied in an image or icon. These services, which comforted the body of the deity, were performed in privacy like daily rituals of worship according to the Agama texts. These temples were not very large and ornate (Figure 3A).

The rangabhoga which included in addition to daily worship rituals the offering of Gita and Vaadya through music, dance and recitation of puranic episodes was meant to please the God. The music and dance as part of worship was open to the public who were attracted to temples to listen to music even before they entered them. The devotees who offered rangabhoga belonged to the promoters of fine arts. This was achieved when rangabhoga services were introduced in temples. Thereafter dance and music became an integral part of daily worship, with dancers living up to the expectations by drawing a huge crowd. A good-looking young dancer with all her attributes and talent was always been sought after by the audience.

Temples which offered rangabhoga had to be large enough with a dancing platform in the Navaranga pillared hall (see Fig.3.C) in front of the garbhagriha which was large to accommodate the audience. The temple premises had to have an attached place called Sulegeri where dancers and other artists who offered services to God could reside. It involved huge money as these artists could not do other types of jobs for their livelihood. Chalukyan rulers believed that, the dance rendered by young and beautiful girls attracted large number of devotees, which probably helped in maintaining harmony in cultural and religious heritage. King Vikramaditya the VI, built the Mahadeva temple at a place called Ittagi (Karnataka) and donated a modest place and money to take care of the dancers who were employed in the temple (Epigraphia Indica, XIII, page 56).

Each sculpture, whether a deity, or apsara as a semi divine or even civilians depicting some activity had to be sculptured in a definite posture, according to the Shilpa sastra. For this, the significance of the deity, the mythological relation, the measurements according to Shilpa shastra and the prescribed dancing postures, had to be studied thoroughly by sthapati and sculptors too. Therefore, the knowledge of Natyashastra became (compulsorily) infused into Shilpa shastra. The Agama shastra gives the characteristic of each sculpture as 'Dhyana shloka' and the sculptor had to visualize and create the meaning of shloka in stone. Indian sculptors who carved dancing figures, were guided by the principle of dance in movement and Dhyana shloka must have been definition of sthaanas (Leg posture), charis (Leg movement in progress) or karanas (combined movement of hands and legs) - as given in Natyashastra. Hence these dance sculptures are the authentic codification of art in stone, practiced, during that period of history. The sculptures which were created according to shastramaana (proportions of symmetry) are truly lovely. Sculptors and sthapatis were so much influenced and inspired by dance that even the act of combing hair , shooting an arrow, pulling a thorn from the sole or afraid of a scorpion in her dress were all portrayed as dancing figures meticulously observing the prescribed rules of expression, the nine sentiments as prescribed in text on dramaturgy Natyashastra. Even the high-ranking deities like Shiva, Ganapathi and Sarasvati, Durga, were all depicted in dancing mode.

6. Paatras (Dancers): A Historical Aspect

With the prolific temple building activities during the Hoysala period, temple art reached the zenith of its glory under the leadership of kings Vishnuvardhana, Narasimha and Ballala, who were great patrons of art. Even though Hoysala temple came out with its own unique style and identity, there were stylistic differences in the various workshops in the Hoysala period. The Cennakeshava temple at Belur built by King Vishnuvardhana in 1117 AD, was the earliest structure constructed in a fully evolved Hoysala style. The temple, which was dedicated to God Vijayanarayana, in celebration of the king's victory over Cholas, reflected his faith in religion and his love for art. His queen Shantaladevi (who died in 1129 A.D) who was also a temple dancer, before her marriage, probably inspired the sculptors to carve out sculptures in dancing postures observing perfect postures. King Vishnuvardhana had many Queens. Shantala and Lakshmidevi were his queens who were well versed in the art of dance and music. Many inscriptions bear testimony for the queen's philanthropic activities. Later the king married Chandaladevi, the daughter of Kongaalva king. Bommala and Raajala were his paramours.

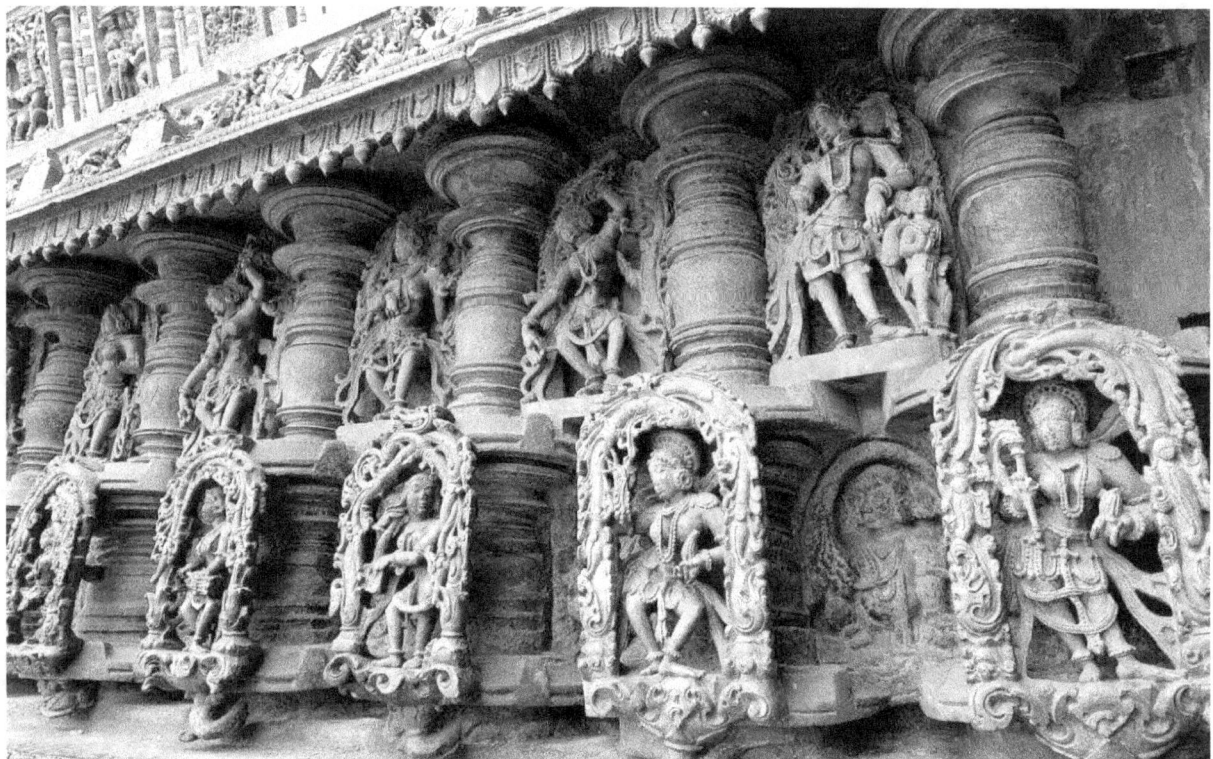

Figure 4: Depiction of Paatras – The temple dancers in the lower bands.

Of the many temples built during that period, Cennakeshava temple at Belur enjoys a special place because of the dancing sculptures of the celestial beauties - the madanikas / Shilabalikas, all of which are well preserved. Looking like Apsaras on the outer walls of the temple, they entertain Gods forever and are a sensual reward for the King, who fought bravely. These apsaras are like permanent records of the unique sculptural style, reflecting the in-depth knowledge of dance and music, which both the dancers and sculptors had, in that period. In medieval period two types of temples evolved – 1. The ones, which gave services of only the worshipping rituals angabhoga, and, 2. Temples that offered a service through dance and music, rangabhoga. The rangabhoga rituals involved great expenditure as the responsibility of hiring and maintaining artists like singers, musicians, flutists, percussionists and dancers came under temple maintenance in addition to the temple cleaners and priests. Besides this, the temple also had an associated place called sulegeri, a place where all these artists resided under the care of a teacher called Sulevala, who taught dance to girls. The rangabhoga temple service, became a popular form of worship during the late Chalukyan and Hoysala periods, attracting many devotees, as it gave them an opportunity to see and enjoy fine arts.

The dancers and sculptors became familiar with Natyashastra, the traditional text on dance and dramaturgy. The dancers who were called "paatra", were also trained to know the intricacies of expressive dance, otherwise called 'abhinaya', as they had to enact lead roles in episodes of puranic stories in temples. These dancers were moulded into the versatility of "nartikis" as described in Natyashastra. The apsara figures of Belur temple are, probably the sculptural representation of paatras, the temple dancers, who rendered dance services every day in a temple. Sculptors were enthusiastic to carve dancing sculptures as they looked more artistic and gave them ample scope to exhibit their skill and served like permanent records of cultural heritage.

Thus, temples, which were mere worshipping places evolved as an indispensable part of the society with various types of responsibilities. They served as centers of religion, education and fine arts, thus promoting the mass and younger generations in the field of education and cultural heritage. It gave employment to teachers, sculptors, priests, dancers, musicians and attendants, through whom the cultural heritage was carried over from generation to generation.

7. The Socio-Religious aspects of Paatras

Dancers, who were called as paatra in Chalukyan inscriptions, who belonged to a separate class in service of God were probably represented as apsaras on the outer walls of the Chalukyan and Hoysala temples. The earlier architectural depiction of apsara to be holding the branch of Shala tree got changed to the Figure being presented in the frame of a flowering bush in Hoysala style of art which gave immense scope for the sculptors to exhibit their skill in intricate carvings. Dancers enjoyed a respectable and good social status. Even the queens of Chalukyan and Hoysala rulers were well trained in the art of dance and music. The popular opinion about these sculptures in Belur temple, is that they represent queen Santala, wife of the Hoysala ruler, who was a paatra before her marriage (Epigraphia Carnatica, V, Belur 58, 1117.A D).

Girls who were young, beautiful and talented were brought either locally or from outside, were looked after well in Sulegeri a special residential place for these artists. Each Sulegeri had a male dance teacher and a caretaker called Sulevala or Natuva, who was well versed with Natyashastra and who trained girls in dancing.

These artists were in general called Devaditi - meaning an ardent servant of God. The Devaditis who were exclusive dancers were called 'Paatras' meaning the main 'role' that is played in a ballet (dance drama). She had to know the rules of pure dance, the art of communication to express the abhinaya (expressive part of dance), and the episodes related to the mythologies and puranas. Paatra had to be young, beautiful, exponent of music and had to undergo vigorous training in dance lessons. The co dancers who performed the side roles were called Nati. The other artists who assisted Paatra's recitals with instruments were Vamshiga (flautist), two Maddalekaras [Percussionists], Gaayaka (a singer), Parekara (an instrumentalist) and so on, who were called Kushilava according to Natyashastra. These Paatras or dancers performed dance, every day in front the main deity, in a raised dancing platform of the assembly hall called Navaranga.

The position of the main dancer Paatra was not always hierarchical. Anybody could learn the art of dancing and become a Paatra, as it was a prestigious and respected position. She enjoyed the special privilege of being the first one to receive 'Prasaada' the blessings of God. It was was not compulsory for Paatra to be in service of temple forever. One of the inscriptions of Belur says about queen Shantala was "Vichirtra nartana pravartana paatra sikhamanium…. sangita sangata Sarasvatium".(Ref."Kalyana Chakukya Devalayagalu Ondu Samskrutika Adhyayana", H.S. Gopal Rao,1993). This confirms that Queen Shantala was a paatra .

The Sulegeri Govindeshwara temple inscription (South Indian inscriptions, IX-1-101, 1018 A.D) gives detailed descriptions of twelve ladies who were employed for dancing in temple along with a teacher and caretaker Natuva. One of the Belur temple inscriptions (Epigraphia Carnatica, V, Belur 58, 1117 A.D) mentions about the queen Shantala, wife of King Vishnuvardhana, who herself was a paatra, was well versed in music and dance. She donated very liberally, to the livelihood of paatra and other artists, rendering the service of rangabhoga. Dancers and musicians thus played a very important role in the temple rituals of rangabhoga temple. The circular dancing platform was almost a part of temple architecture of Chalukyan and Hoysala era. The rulers, through the media of paatra, enjoyed the essence of art and provided the unique opportunity to a large section of pilgrims to watch the performance and thus indirectly educated the public about our rich cultural heritage.

8. Paatras - The Nartakis of Natyashastra, depicted as Apsara Sculptures

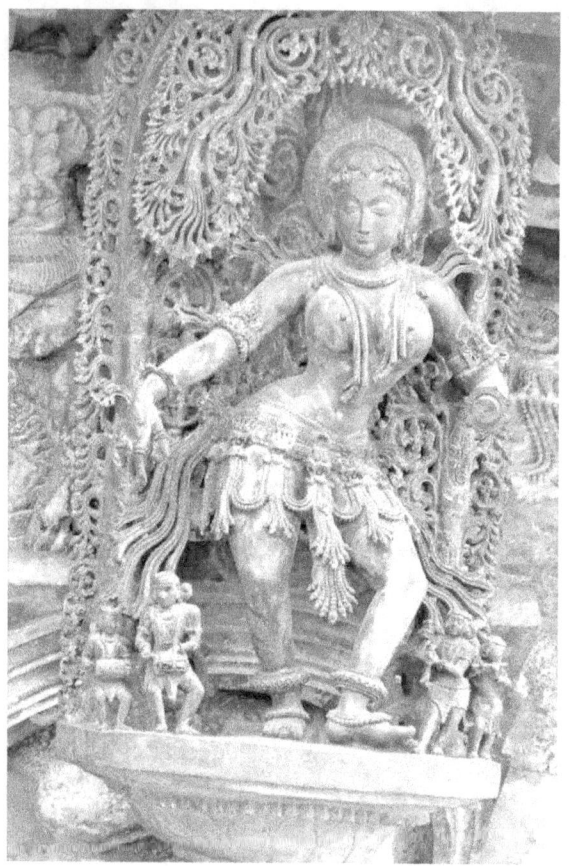 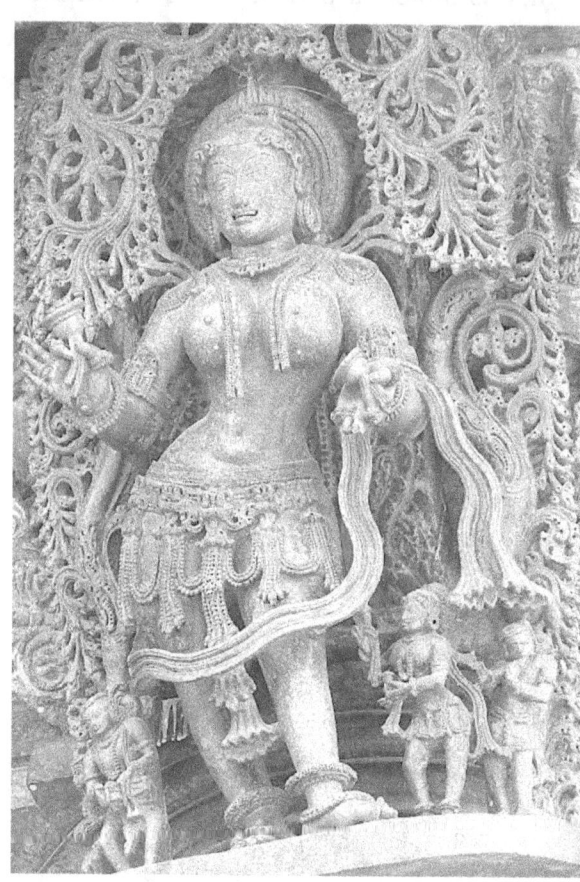

Figures 5A and 5B: Nartaki depicted as apsara on oval shaped lotus base

The facial features of the shilabalikas as apsaras differ from figure to figure. It can be inferred by the study of Natyashastra and Manasollasa that the main dancer paatra and co dancer nati as performing artists of Chalukyan period were groomed like nartaki of Natyashastra. Probably paatras were the role models for sculptors - of the Chalukyan and Hoysala era to make the figures of dancers. Apsara sculptures of Belur Chennakeshava temple are carved according to the lakshanas of nartaki. According to the Natyashastra (Ch. 34 Sl. 50-54), a nartaki should be delicate in appearance, pleasant in looks, intelligent, polite and modest. She should be with inborn qualities of a dancer - like good voice, beautiful physique, thorough knowledge of various instruments and music; proficiency in 64 types of arts. She must be a lady without any physical deformity, always active without getting tire, proficient in dance, music, signing. She should catch the attention of public by her looks, and qualities. Manasollasa in many stanzas describe the women to be young, beautiful, with slender waist, full breasts and well-dressed who can attract large crowd.

The figures appear to be the true representations of the queens who might have been like paatras of Chalukyan and Hoysala era visualized with the personality of a nartaki of Natyashastra. The permanent sculptural record of paatras and their elevated status was carved as apsaras on a lotus pedestal as bracket figures in Belur temple. These sculptures are perennially attracting devotees and propagating our art form. The concept that was conceived by Chalukyan and Hoysala rulers has stood the test of time and are still attracting people from all over the world. Many forts and palaces built by the same rulers are seen in a ruined state, but the temples have remained intact because of the aspect of fine art that was involved.

 Apsaras the everlasting youthful dancers mainly depict the cultural and social heritage and thus invite the attention of pilgrims to holy shrines. Their main role was confined to herald the art and architecture, with special emphasis on dance and music. In Indian temple dancing sculptures, both feminine and masculine forms were frequently idealized. The slim waist, heavy breasts, lithe limbs, youthful sensuous poise was the outcome of idealized feminine grace moulded in the frame of shastra mana. Manasollasa also has similar description of women who were dear to the king. The belief that the measurements of human body as prescribed in Agamas, ought not to be disregarded under any circumstance, came into vogue during this period also. The artist was thus handicapped with less freedom of action, and imagination or variation in body proportions were not entertained. The genius of the artist, regarding his imaginary skills, took a second place while making an image. He was hard struck with the rules of Agamas and he could fashion the images as best as he could within the framework of Agamas. The departure from the rules laid down authoritatively in Shastras was not easily tolerated. Hence, they look different from Greek or Roman sculptures, which are close to human anatomy. However, Hoysala apsaras kept the proportion closer to realism than the Chalukyan dance figures, where the limbs are over emphasized with long proportions. Even through the jewelry is in no way very different from the jewelry used by the current Odissi or Bharatanatyam performing dancers, apsaras look over decked because of their short stature and the medium of stone.

Apsaras are more than successful in bringing out the glory of the past. These figures of artists hint that dance and music were deep rooted among Indians much before they were expressed as dancing sculptures. The diplomatic ways in which the Hoysala rulers-maintained harmony and tolerance in religious sects and managed to get continued patronage and support from public through dancers, speak volumes on the capacity of the dynastic rulers. Equally well the paatras or nartakis glorified as apsaras herald the rich heritage and tradition of our culture, which differentiated Indian temples from those in other countries.

9. The Dwarf Attendants of Nartaki

The bracket figures of Belur temple shows different themes. If one shows parrot on hand the other one is with bow and arrows. Yet another one displays her long hair. Even though there are four figures with the theme of birds and three figures with bow and arrow, the panels are not placed in a sequence or progression of the same activity. Each bracket Figure has many types of attendants as dwarf figures at the base helping to support the activity of the main sculpture indirectly. Of the 42 figures, 24 figures depict either music or dance recitals in which the dwarf attendants are both in male and female genders. The accompanying artists playing instruments, co dancers or singers are all depicted in the same height. The male artists in general are called vaisheshika (trained in fine arts) in Natyashastra and female co artists are nati or nataka stri.

The 18 thematic figures depict social themes, has dwarf attendants of only female category playing different roles in support of the activity that the apsara is depicting. Their varied status and intimacy with the main Figure are directly proportional to the height of dwarf figures in relation to the main Figure. Lowest status is the shortest Figure is carved half the knee length while higher intimacy is almost up to the navel region of the main Figure. It is only because of a strict adherence to the rules of shastra mana that even the dwarf sculptures look proportionate, most delectable and artistic in bringing out the buoyant spirit of music, dance or other arts. They help to recognize the oneness of Indian Sculptors with texts related to Shilpa shastra, and Natyashastra.

The messenger or an attendant of a heroin or queen is called duti in Sanskrit. The actions or the role played by the various attendant images, their status and their decorations vary according to the theme of the panels. When apsara is dressing, the attendants as daasi help her with more jewelry, when she is with a parrot, they offer fruits. When she is dancing or singing, they are co dancers or singers and when apsara is engrossed in a hunting or archery game they are supplying more arrows or support in associated work. They perfectly match the Duti Lakshana or the various types of attendants a nartaki / heroine can enjoy. According to Natyashastra, (Ch 25, 9-11) and Dasharoopaka (Part 2; 46) which mentions 8 types of Dutis.

"Dutyo Daasi Sakhi Kaarur Dhatreyi Prativeshika,
Lingini shilpini Svam cha, Netramitro gunanvita".

The basic quality of duti should be netramitro gunanvita - pleasant to look, shrewd and intelligent. Duti must be supportive to her mistress. She must accompany her in festivals, in gardens and other places and create an opportunity for the heroine and hero to meet. She must be good-looking and be able to maintain secrecy of her mistress. It is interesting to observe that all the eight types of attendants are depicted as the dwarf figures of apsara panels.

In allocation of work, an attendant or duti may be:

Daasi is an attendant - female servant who help apsara in all her activities. They are carved up to knee length of the main Figure, appear pleasant in status by wearing more jewelry as seen on the left side of the main Figure 6.A and 6.E.

Sakhi – Companion,a female friend. Sakhi is carved upto the hip level of apsara. She is the tallest among attendants as seen in Figure 6.G. indicating more intimacy. They appear slim and young but with less jewellery and without Yajnopavita and are present where apsara is with a parrot.

Kaaru - Servant who does menial jobs. Kaaru is shortest in the group of attendants - half the knee height of the main Figure (as seen in 6.A and 6.B). They wear minimum jewelry and are stout and fat, doing menial jobs like cleaning, carrying the pet animal monkey, etc.

Dhatreyi (Stepmother is Dhatri and step sister is Dhatreyi) appears equally well dressed as a apsara. She is carved up to hip level, as seen in 6.A and right-side attendant of Fig. 6.H. where apsara is admiring herself in a mirror. Only dhatreyi wears a yagnopavita, like the main Figure indicative of higher status.

Prativeshika – neighbor is like sakhi as seen in Fig. 6.B or 6 H.

Lingini - an attendant who is literate, and well-versed in sastras. Lingini is an attendant seen in 6.F, are slightly above knee level up to thigh region of the main figures and appear modest and serious by nature as they are literate and well versed in sastras. They are well dressed like natis.

Shilpini - Attendant who is skilled in different arts. Shilpini is like a daasi in stature but helps apsara in sporting or special activities as seen in 6.C, or like in Fig.7, hunting activity by giving more arrows.

Svam - The heroine herself plays the role of attendant.

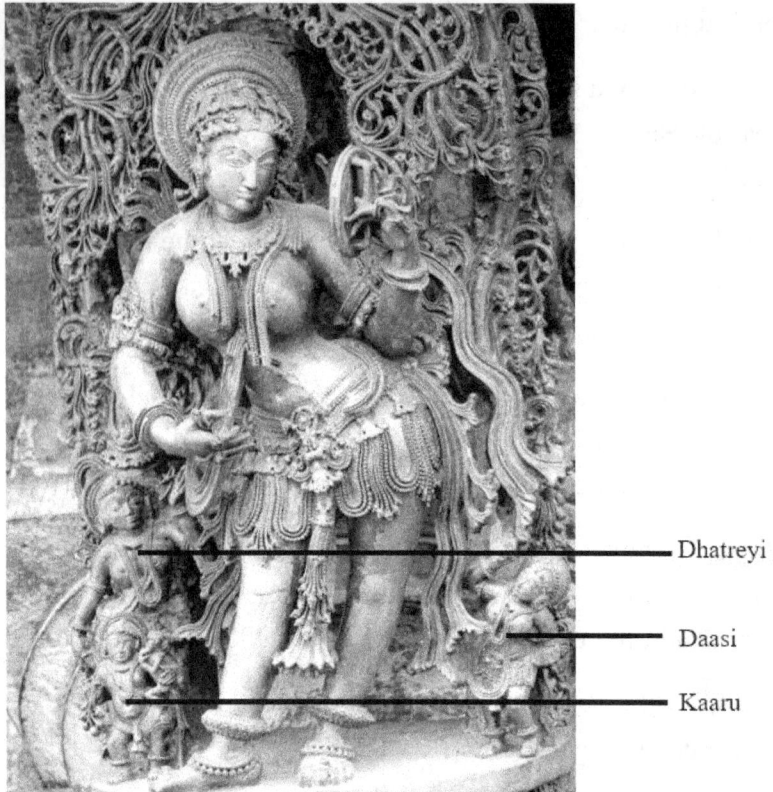

Dhatreyi

Daasi

Kaaru

Figure 6A

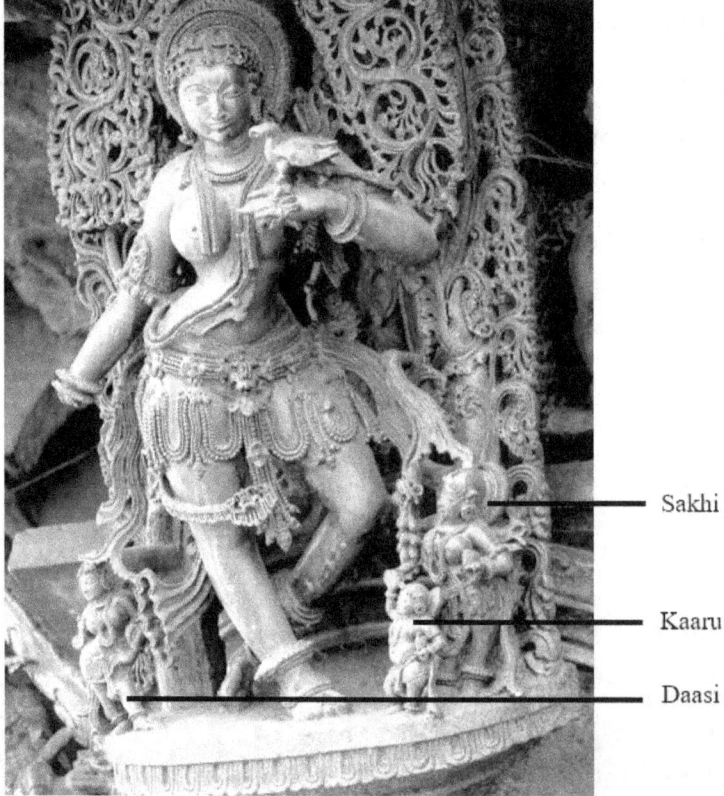

Sakhi

Kaaru

Daasi

Figure 6B

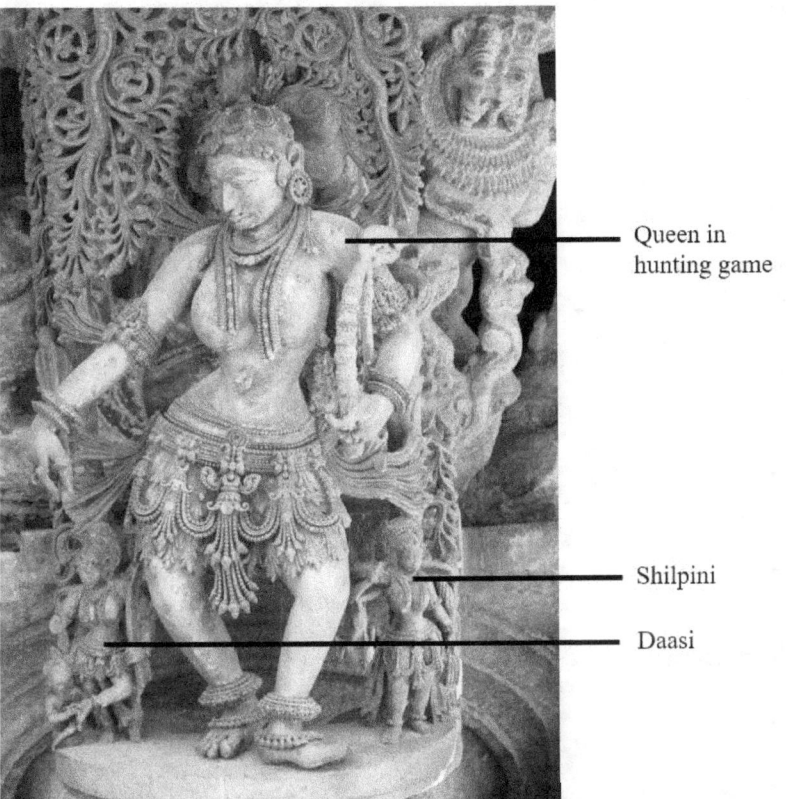

Queen in
hunting game

Shilpini

Daasi

Figure 6C

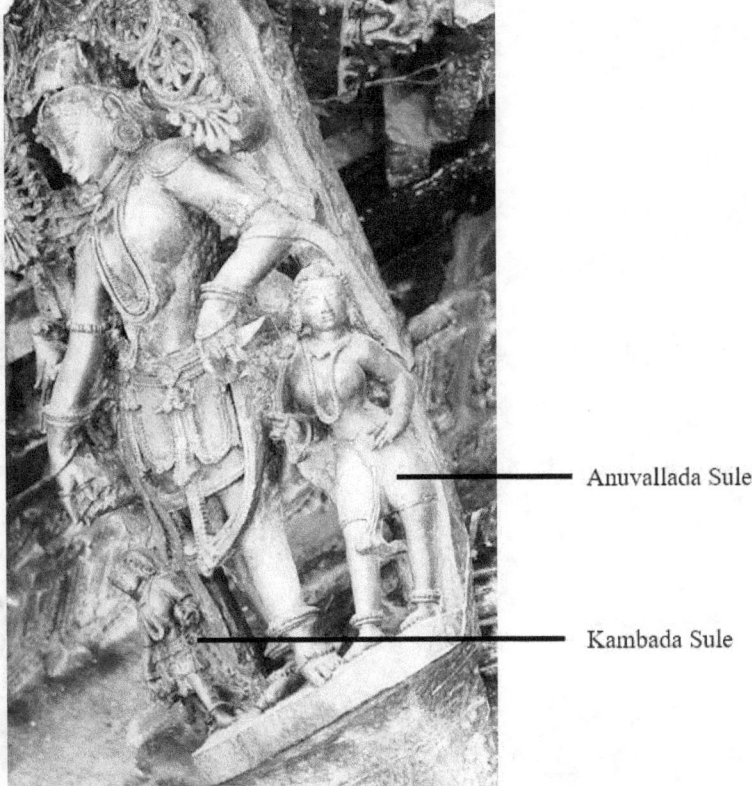

Anuvallada Sule

Kambada Sule

Figure 6D

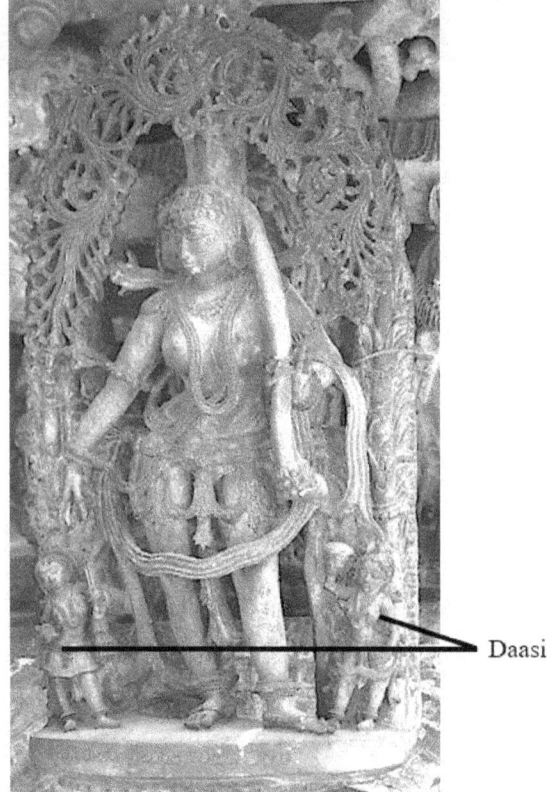

Daasi

Figure 6E

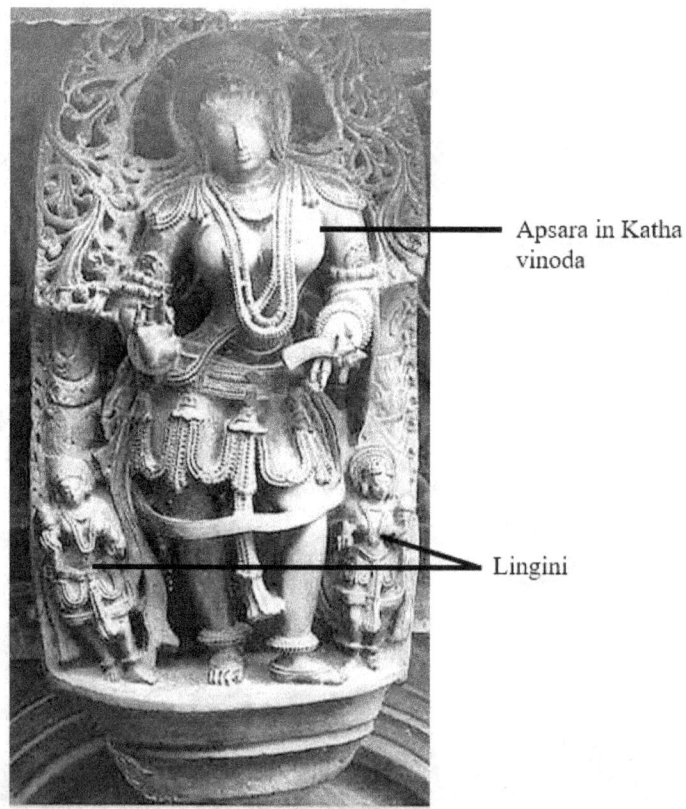

Apsara in Katha
vinoda

Lingini

Figure 6F

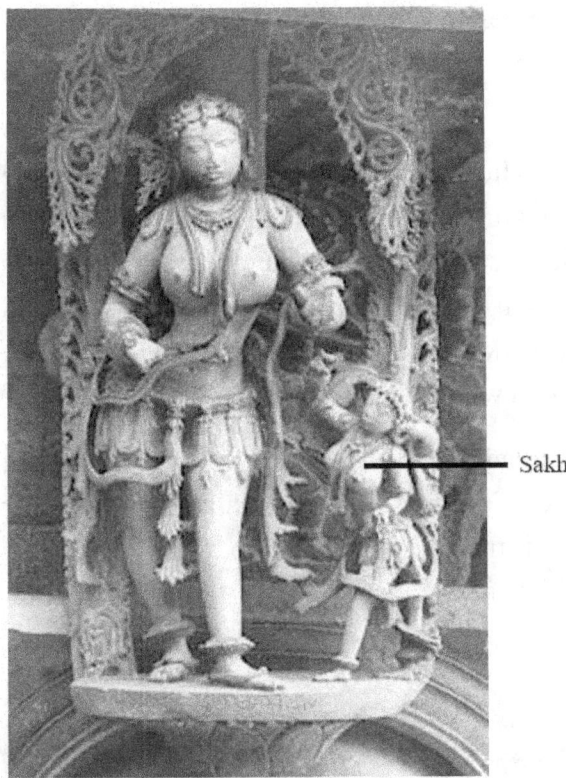

Figure 6G

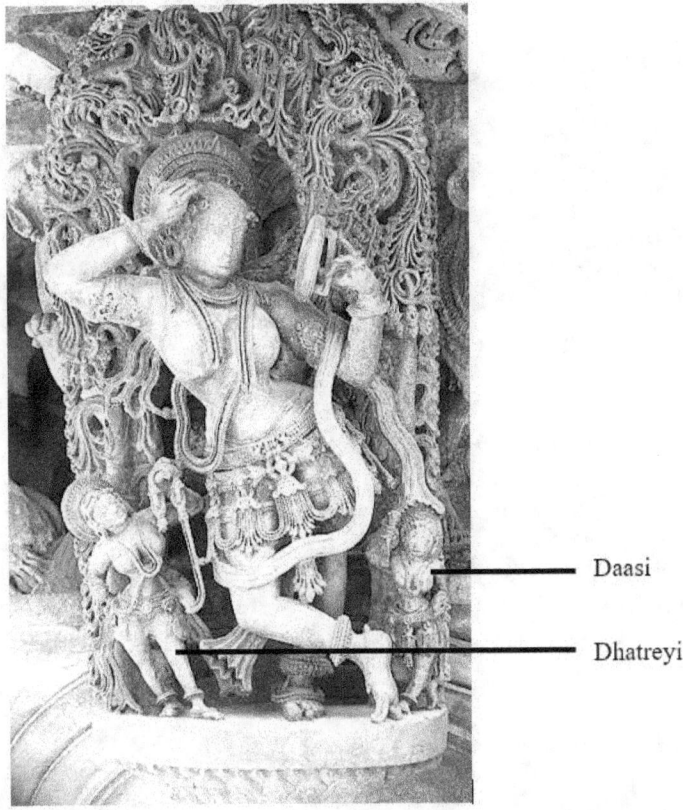

Figure 6H

Figures 6A-H: Identification of the type of Daasi present in the apsara sculptures of Belur temple.

The inscriptions of temples and Manasollasa has many references regarding the main dancer and the attendants. They are addressed with a slightly different term than Natyashastra though the roles played were similar.

Daasi - was called a Sule in inscriptions. Sule or daasi's allocated work was maintaining the temple clean. She also assisted the paatra in her toilette and in all other activities like hunting. Sule was a general term for the attendants like lingini, shilpini, daasi or sakhi, played multiple roles. Sules were of two types, one who stood with a chaamara or fan was a chaamarasule and one who stood by the side of a kamba (pillar) and assisted in other work was kambadasule as seen in Fig. 6.D. They had further specification of right and left side ones with different work to do.

'Kumari'or kanya in Natyashastra was called anuvalladasule- an innocent very young girl in temple inscriptions. She could probably be the daughter of prativeshika - a neighbor, or stepmother dhatreyi. She can be compared to a friendly sakhi. She is the tallest in the group of attendants, (see Fig. 6.D) depicting more intimacy that paatra had with her.

10. The Versatility of Hoysala Queens

Hoysala queens enjoyed varieties of indoor and outdoor games. The queens relaxed by engaging themselves in various outdoor and indoor activities depending on the season and climatic condition, besides their involvement in the field of music and dance. Their activities are described in Manasollasa and Some of them can be seen in the bracket Figure sculptures. It can also be interpreted that the King Vishnuvardhana had many wives, each one being good in some art, sport or literature which were documented in stone medium as sculptures.

Sculptures were used as a media to express the thought process, be it in the field of fine arts or in the field of philosophy. Natyasastra was used as a "sutra"- a base or foundation, on which social, mythological and philosophical aspects manifested as structure. The result of the influence of Natyashastra is reflected in the projection Hindu Gods, mythological personalities and the apsaras- all represented in dancing modes. Even the social theme of a queen's enthusiasm in archery, or her joyous moments are depicted in a dance mode, in stone, meticulously observing the leg, hand and head positions, costumes and accessories that can be used, as laid out in Natyasastra.

10.1 Dhanurvidya – Archery

Archery the outdoor game which the women enjoyed is beautifully described in Manasollasa. Women specialized in Archery – a heroic sport that developed heroic spirit. The science of Archery was inevitable in warfare.

Women of royal families were also trained to use bow and arrow, as they often accompanied the king in the game of archery. A woman, shooting arrows was a favorite theme of sculptors in Chalukyan and Hoysala era. The skill in archery the queen accomplished was depicted in stone, through a lady shooting arrows at bull's eye, or a lady shooting an arrow from a mobile platform. One of the apsaras sculptures at the Belur temple, (see Figure 7), depicts a lady in a heroic posture, shooting arrows at birds or at an animal in higher level. These sculptures indicate the interest women had in Archery. The lady is with an assistant who is carrying a bundle of arrows. She is called "shilpini" for she was also good at archery and knew what type of arrow was to be given.

The archer is depicted to be standing in the heroic posture called "alidha sthana" where the right leg is extended back by 3 talas. The posture is employed in the acts of heroic sentiments, self-confidence, release of weapons, wrestlers act and so on. Bow string was to be pulled up to the ear level before releasing the arrow according to Manasollasa. The release of arrow is depicted in the figure. The bow which the women use is smaller than the ones used by men folk according to Manasollasa.

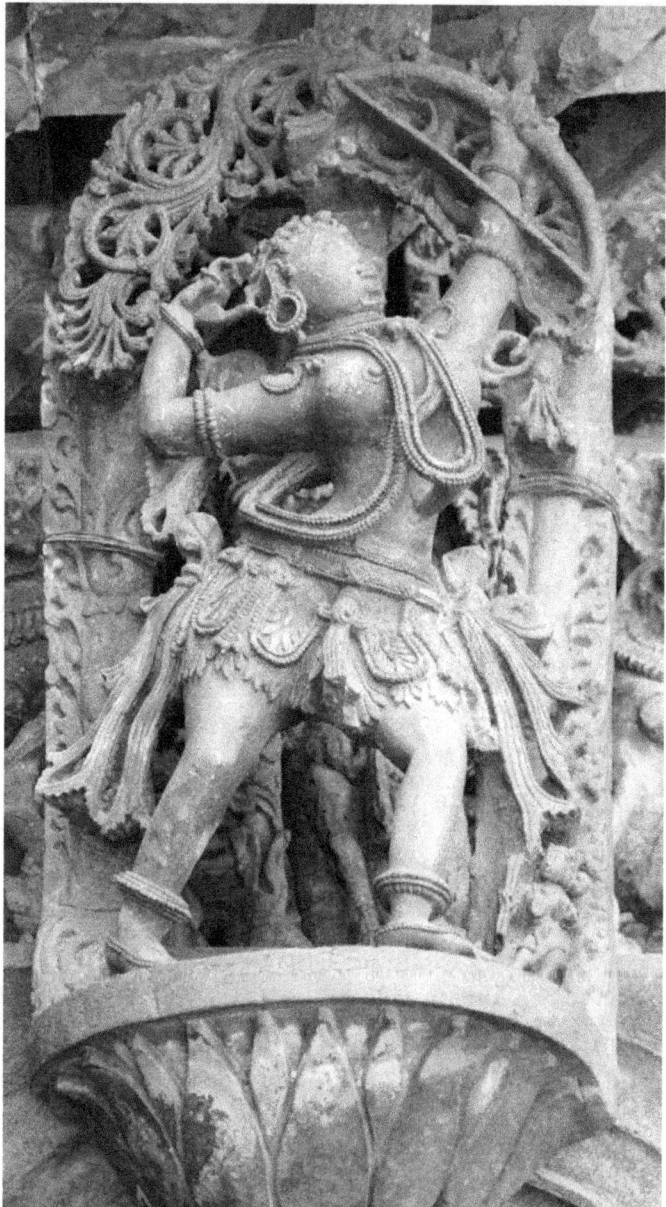

Figure 7: Apsara engrossed in archery.

10.2 Mrigaya Vinoda – The Hunting Game

The 15th chapter of 4th vimsati of Manasollasa has details of 31varieties of hunting games classified as "Mrigaya vinoda" that the royal people enjoyed hunting as a sport in winter season. Royal families hunted in a reserve forest, not far from the city and which was free from fierce animals but contained sober ones like deer, sambar, rabbits, peacock and varieties of birds. King, queen and co hunters, attendants were all dressed in green colored costumes and head decorations. Paaniyaja, Dipa mriga, Maargaja, Chaaraja, Oosharaja were some types of hunting games in which queens participated. Queens sometimes accompanied the king in hunting expeditions and sometimes went with co hunters in the private gardens. Much before the royal family went for hunting expedition, hiding shelters were made ready either on tree tops or an artificial shelter made by digging earth at lower level and laid with cushions made of grass. These were arranged near the paths usually used by animals near water sources and the game was called maargaja. Animals which came to drink water were hunted. Some games were also with a spread of soaked chick peas or gram and fresh greens in open area and royal families hunted in moon lit days. Of the several hunting games, a few called dipa mriga and paaniyaja are depicted in bracket figures.

Dipa Mrigaja: Royal women, dressed in green short costumes called "dvipadis", enjoyed the hunting expeditions in the reserve forest. The text Manasollasa gives the details of a hunting game called "dipa mrigaja" that was in vogue during those days. A young healthy female deer was trained and made into bait – called "dipa mriga". Dipa in Sanskrit means to shine, to rouse and that which excites and stimulates. Such a deer was trained to respond to signal calls and taken to the forest with a rein like that of a horse (See Figure below where the daasi is holding the dipa mriga deer with the leash around its neck). The trained deer was taken to the reserve forest and released to mix with the wild ones. After some time, the signal call was given to the trained deer which would run to the master. The trained young deer was followed by the wild pack of deer which were then hunted.

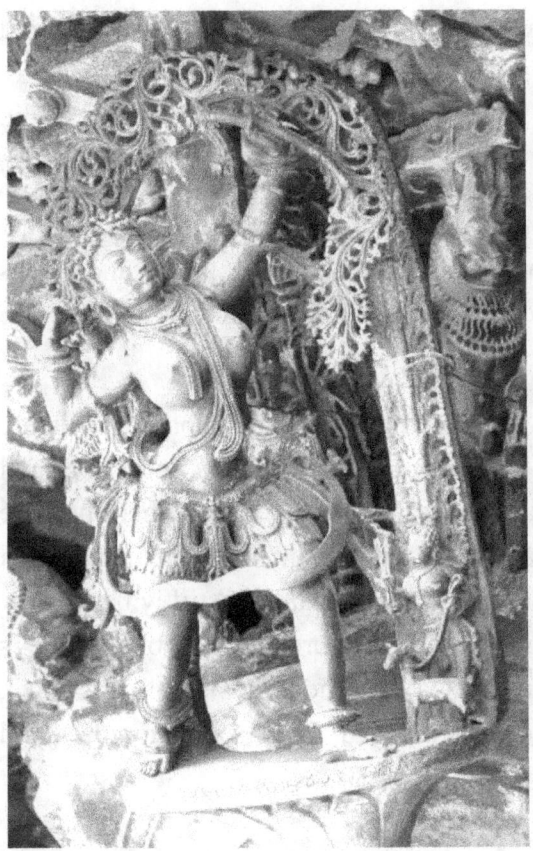 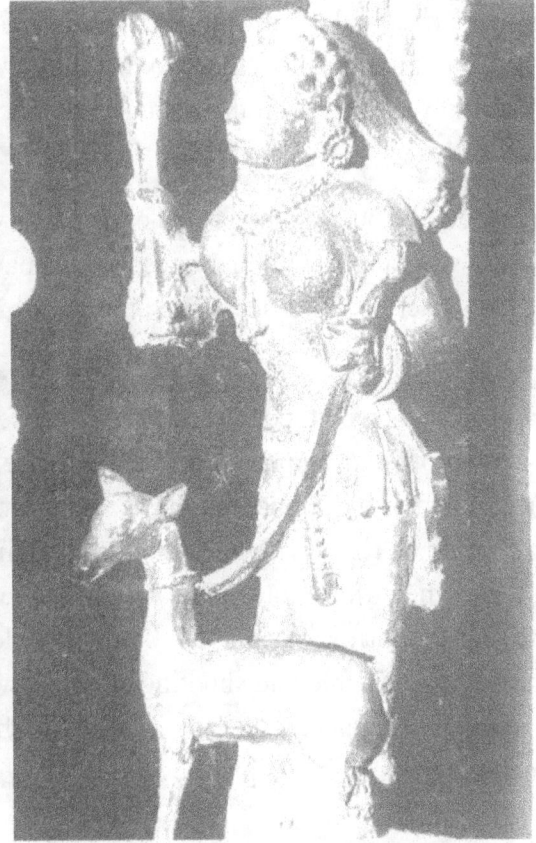

Figure 8A   Figure 8B

Figure 8A: Apsara engrossed in the hunting game dipa mriga. Figure 8B: The assistant shilpini supplying more arrows holds the dipa mriga in the leash.

The lady in Figure 8A, shooting the arrow upwards which indicates she was waiting in the shelter dug at a lower place. She is shooting the arrow to a higher level. The dipa mriga or the trained young deer is seen with the reins which has come back to the master. The assistant shilpini, a co hunter in Figure 8B is holding it in the left hand, and she holds a bundle of arrows in the right hand. The co hunter is also dressed in a short, green colored dvipadi, with leafy decoration. The queen is seen with a "brahma sutra" - the sacred thread, that is indicative of a higher social status, which the co hunter is not wearing.

10.3 Paniyaja – Hunting Game

Another hunting game, the Manasollasa describes is the "Paniyaja". On moonlit nights the royal couple or queen with her associates would go to the forest. wait near water places concealed in the hollow of trees or wait in a shelter dug for the royal people to hide. In the sculpture Figure. 9, the lady is seen waiting with the bow and arrow. Hunting was a strenuous game and ladies often got hurt in their foot. First aid was given by a hunting partner. On the right side we can see the partner massaging or dressing the hurt foot. Transportation of the game was also strenuous. Carcass of hunted deer had to be cleared immediately so that the wild pack are not in doubt of humans around. The legs of the dead animals were tied and hung on either side of the pole. In Figure 9.B, the hunted animals, a deer and a big water bird are being carried by an attendant. They were cleared first from the area of animal movement so that other wild animals do not doubt about the smell of blood and later they carried it on their shoulders. The attendant on the left, is carrying the game that were hunted.

Near water source like pond, hiding spots or a shelter were created by digging the earth where the king and queens would hide with the trained deer dipa mriga. Soaked chick peas, gram and greens were spread to attract the wild deer. The animals which came for a drink or for the grains were hunted.

Wild deer and animals would come near water source and get attracted by the dipa mriga eating the soaked and sprouted chickpeas. The deer with the leash would indicate by its neck, hoof and tail movement whether the animal that has come to drink water is a wild one or a sober one. The group hiding would be ready with bow and arrow, remain silent without any movement and shoot the animals when they drink water. The above picture shows the lady standing still with the bow ready in left hand and arrow in right hand. Since her looks are down wards it could be that she is hiding in the hollow of a tree and shooting arrow downwards. When the target is at higher level, bow aimed upwards, it indicates the lady is hiding in the shelter dug for them near water place and she is aiming at the animal in a higher level.

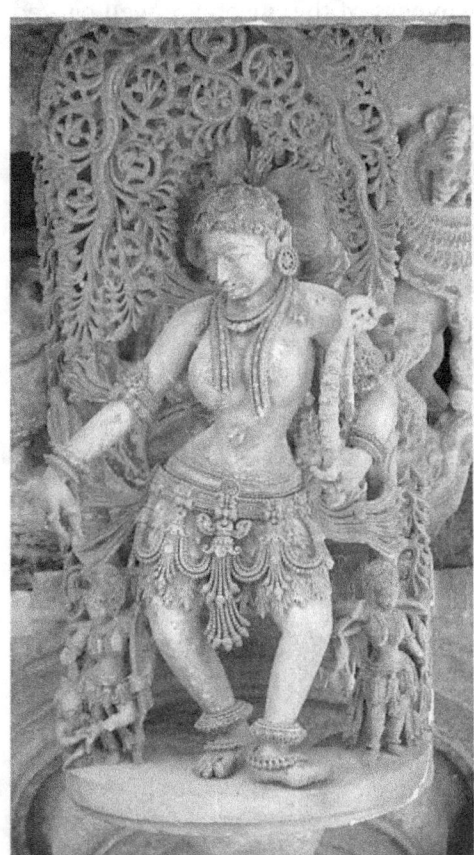 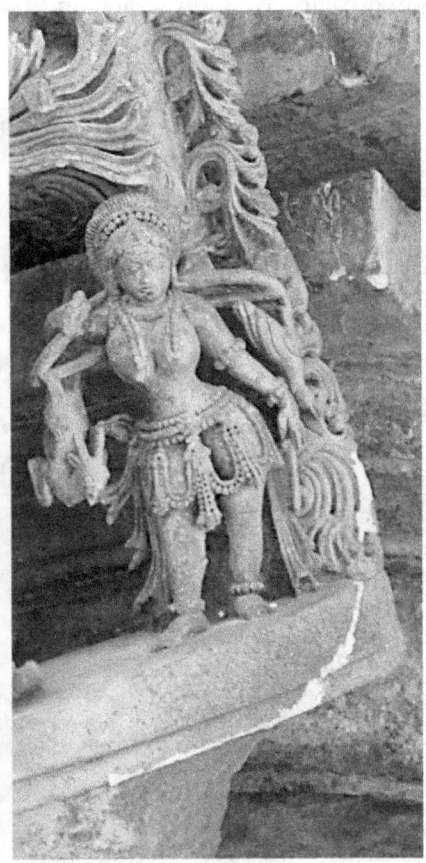

Figure 9A   Figure 9B

Figure 9A and 9B: Apsara in a hunting game Paniyaja. Figure 9B: Enlarged portion of Figure 9A that depicts the carrying of a dead deer and a bird

Another similar game was called dhvanija. Dhvani means a call. The royal family would take shelter in the fruit bearing tree that deers usually like. The attendant hunters would imitate the call of the deer that attracts the pack of wild deers that were hunted.

10.4 Vana kride and Madirapaana kride: Pleasure in a garden

Vana kride is described as a pas time pleasure in a garden. Kride means a sport, pastime play. Someswara in Manasollasa describes how the royal women enjoyed in a garden that was at a suitable distance, from their palace. Different kinds of fruit bearing trees, like mango, jack fruit, banana, pomegranate, and scented flower plants like jasmine, champaka, bakula, were planted and maintained in the "Vana" – the garden. The king and queen used to sport there for pleasure with select members of the harem. Manasollasa describes in detail about vana kride for how the king dressed and looking like Indra would enter the garden alone and enjoy his private time with beautiful women dressed like apsaras (see Figure 10A and 10B) He would roam about with his loved ones showing the best places and trees. They played entertaining games like hide and seek and king enjoyed the intimacy of his preferred paramour in the garden as seen in Figure 10A and

Figure 10B. The pleasant expression on king's face and the shyness of the queen are well carved in the panel.

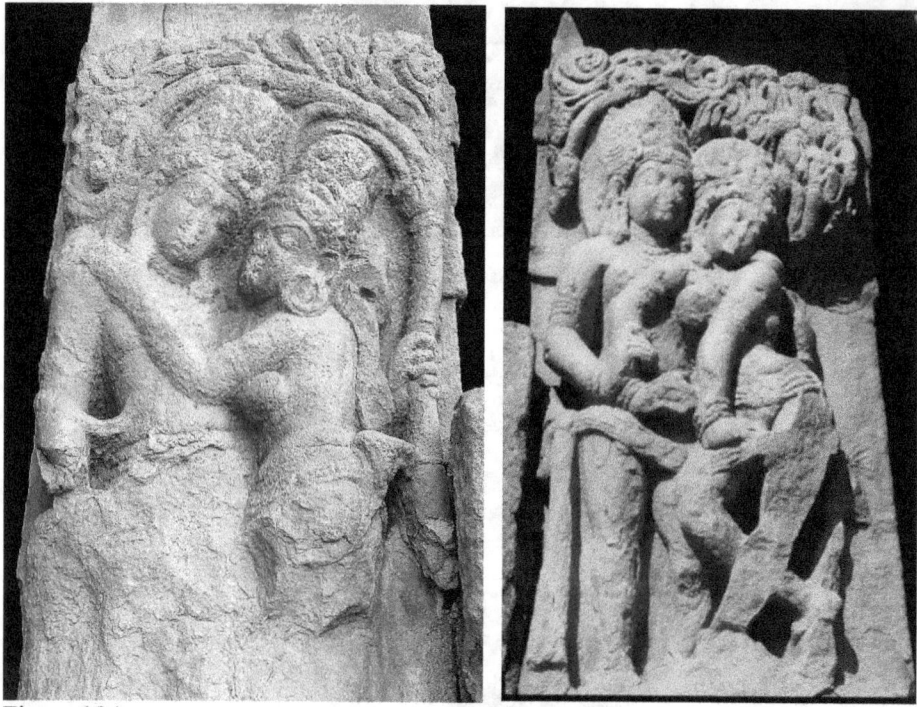

Figure 10A   Figure 10B

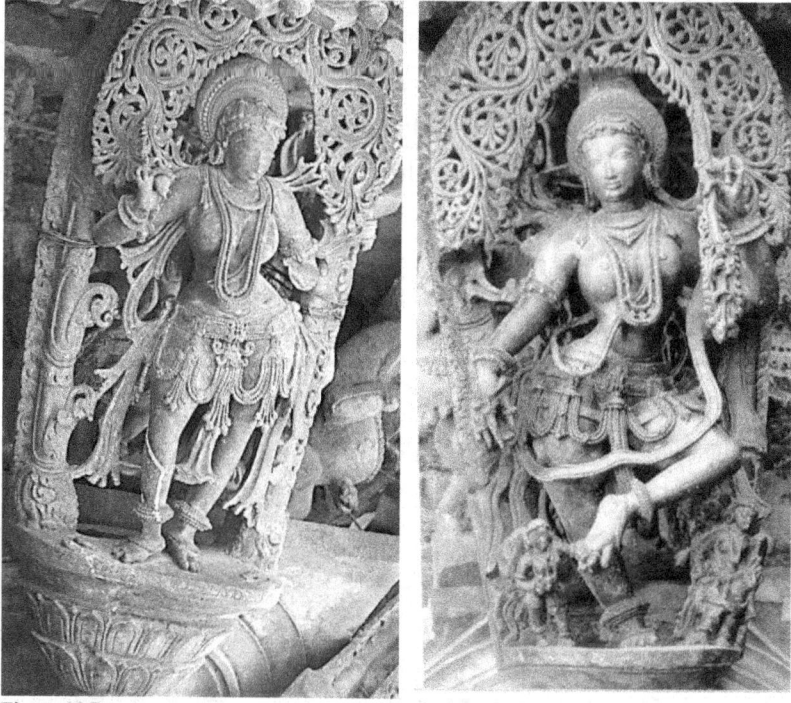

Figure 10C   Figure 10D

Figures 10A-D: Figure 10A and 10B: King enjoying the company of his queen in the garden. Figure 10C: Queen plucking the fruit. Figure 10D: Queen getting her foot examined for the hurt.

Royal women relished fruits which they could choose and pluck. Apsara sculpture in Figure 10C indicates a queen plucking a fruit. Queens enjoyed the act of pulling the branches and plucking the ripe fruits by themselves. Women often encountered a hurt on their foot as they strolled or played hide and seek in the garden with the king. First aid was given by her assistants. Figure 10D indicates a queen whose foot is being examined for the hurt by a daasi. Queen is resting in a posture called Ekapada, (where movement is stopped) taking support from a creeper. Lata griha – was a shelter surrounded with creepers, where varieties of aromatic flower plants and creepers were grown. In spring season, royal women plucked the flowers and buds. Flowers were woven into garlands or bouquets. They decorated themselves and the king with variegated floral ornaments on ears, hair, wrist and neck. The king would also decorate his favorite women with flowers and garlands made by him and enjoyed the songs sung by them. The members of royal families would relax on green grass area, enjoy eating the roasted meat with roasted fresh corn, varieties of fresh legumes roasted in fire and mixed with chillies and lemon in the forest as part of vana kride.

Madirapaana Kride:

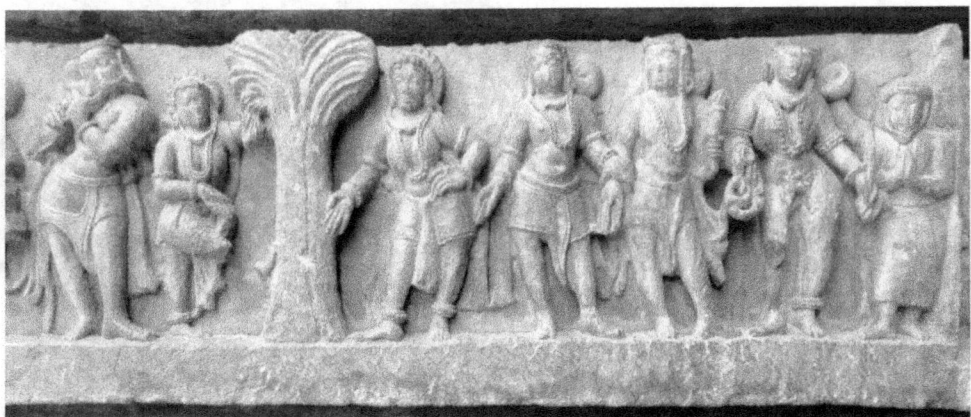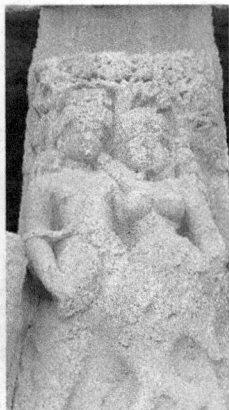

Figure 10E   Figure 10F

Figure 10E: Madirapaana kride. Figure 10F: The royal couple in intoxication.

The 5th chapter in Manasollasa on madira kride details how the royal family enjoyed madirapaana – enjoying the intoxicating drink at a garden or under the shade of a tree covered by an enclosure either as part of vana kride or as a separate kride. In Figure 10D, the lady is extracting the 'sura' from a palm tree. She is also kicking the tree with her right foot with the belief that trees bear more flowers when kicked by a young maiden (Manasollasa). This would be mixed with varieties of fermented fruit juice and other ingredients and enjoyed along with the spicy meat preparation as depicted in the first figure. The intoxicated king is being supported by other family members. The women's imbalanced behavior under intoxication (see Figure 10E) seeing the container as flower or snake and uttering incoherent words are described in detail in 5th chapter. One person looking like a priest (called vita) in his long gown is offering the vessel of madira to a lady and has folded his hands in anjali mudra requesting her to cooperate. The king silently observes the vita / sanyasi's behavior and moves to a woman with round breasts in intoxication. Surata kride of 5th vimshati is about the ways how the king enjoys with young women.

10.5 Aquatic Sports – Jala kride

Dharagriha: To beat the heat of summer and temperature soaring up due to forest fires, the royal family cooled themselves by enjoying water games either in artificial pond called dharagriha or on river side. The alternate places were the temple tanks with lotus called pushkarini or the auspicious pool called Kalyani where arrangements were made. Dharagriha was an artificial lake constructed to beat the heat of summer. Mechanical showers, artificial waterfalls, water jets, streams of water gushing from sprouts of various animal models, were arranged for the enjoyment of royal families. Water was lifted from Step well, filtered and used to fill dharagriha. Somesvara gives a detailed description of curtains that were dropped to cover the area where jala kride was arranged. Around the dharagriha, tents were also made for relaxation.

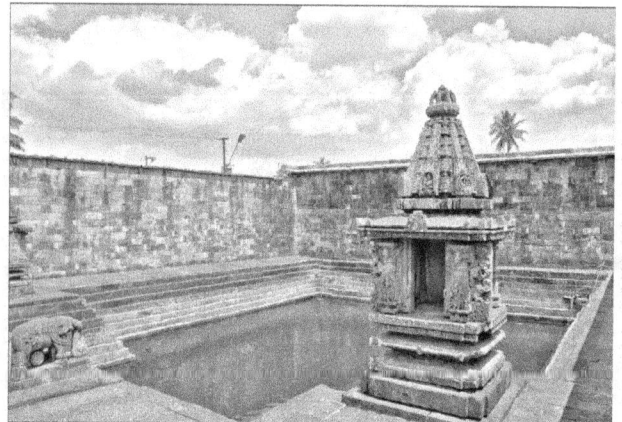 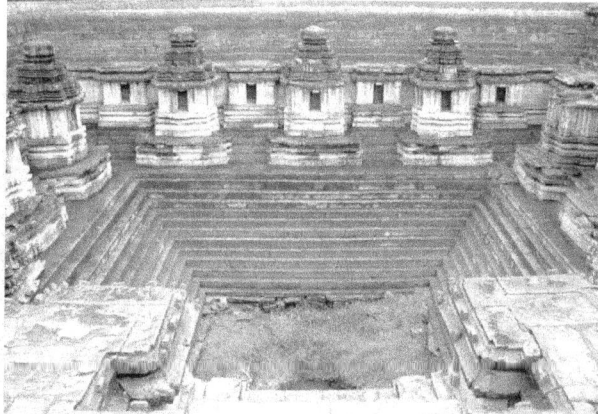

Figure 11: Pushkarini of Belur temple, Kalyani at a Hoysala temple at Hulikere.

Pushkarini was usually square in shape with decorated steps on all sides and surrounded by trees was chosen which could hold neck deep water with aquatic birds and fishes in it. Many beautiful women well dressed in jewels and flowers were also invited for participation. A person well versed in aquatic games would throw slabs of camphor, perfumed flowers to make the water pleasantly perfumed. The young girls would dive and search to locate camphor slabs. Manasollasa compares the well-dressed women moving in water to the moving lotuses. King would later throw small ornaments, precious stones or gold coins (called Nishka in Manasollasa) in the middle of the pond and young girls would show great enthusiasm to find them. The king would embrace whom so ever he liked and enjoys their company in water. Jala kride, a game of Shringara rasa, the sentiment of pleasure would come to an end before sun set. All participants would then dress up again to receive precious and valuable gifts like silk cloth, silk saree or jewels from the king.

Jala sechana kride:

Another such summer time game was "sechana kride" where both men and women sprinkled water on each other. The victory in the war and during spring time was celebrated by sechana kride as post lunch entertainment. The king invited the distinguished personalities from all walks of life, to participate in it. All the priests, ministers, feudatory, brave soldiers' wealthy merchants, writers, musicians, dancers all were invited to participate. Cold and perfumed water was stored in big containers, made of gold and silver. Suitable syringe, made of gold, silver or cow's horn were made and small pots were kept ready to spurt water. The game was inaugurated by the young and beautiful women, dressed in all jewellery and white clothes, sprinkling perfumed and coloured water with red, yellow, sandal, and chandana on the king. Later the entire crowd participated in the game. In the Figure 12, a lady is enjoying spurting water from a syringe. To her left, a man is filling the syringe with colour water, from a big container. Another man is throwing a pot of water on the lady. It is interesting to note that the men and women played together without inhibitions, sprinkling water on one another. The colours were made of natural products like turmeric, kesari, Chandana, herbal colours and water was made fragrant with the extract of flowers, flower petals, camphor and sandal.

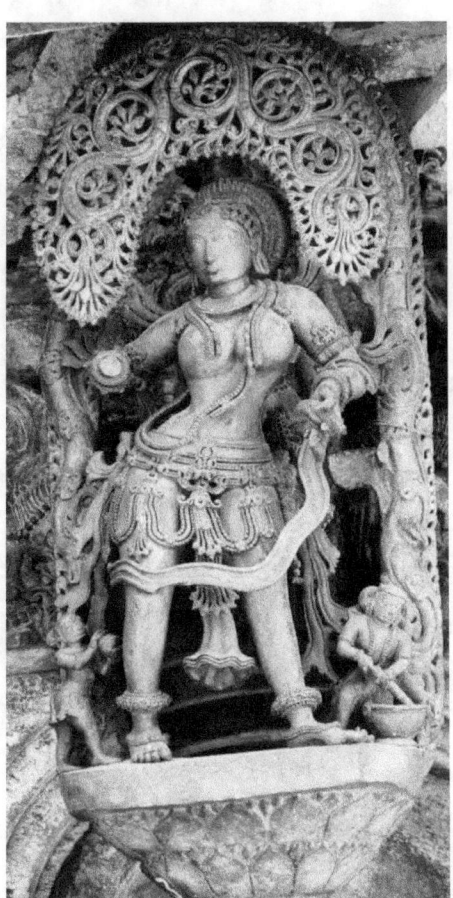

Figure 12. Depiction of sechana kride

The other classics like 'Yasas tilaka' and 'Akhynaka – manikosha' also describe how the heat of summer was beaten by the king playing with royal women in Dharagriha. After enjoying sechana kride the queen and other beautiful women would squeeze water from her hair, re decorate and would assemble to watch various games of animal fights.

10.6 Prema Kride

The King who has been compared to Kubera in wealth and Manmatha in his looks would present himself with best garments and ornaments. Looking like Indra, he would take a round in his city mounted on a decorated elephant or a horse. The queens and beautiful women of harem and paramours called Vilasini would try to attract the king by their decorations. Manasollasa describes how royal women dressed for this occasion and the Belur panels depict how enthusiastically they tried different types of hair styles and decorations to attract him.

One displays her naturally beautiful long hair with keshajaala net and pearly decoration to attract the king (Figure 13A and 13B). Her daasis are holding "Veni guccha" -the garland of perfumed flowers. The lady is trying to draw the attention of the king by making pleasant sound of her anklets (observe the foot of Figure 13B) and gazing at him with wide opened eyes. In another panel (Figure 13C) the queen is halfway through her dressing up. She is trying to know which type of ear rings looks better by looking at herself in the mirror which the attendant is holding. The other daasi holds "veniguccha" for her further decoration.

In yet another panel (Figure 13D) the lady is in a hurry to look her best with the hair tied into a bun style called "Kumbhi Bandhaka". In anxiety she has dropped the stud of her ear ornament which the daasi to her left has located and giving her.

(Figures 13E and 13F) Two other panels depict women who believe in profuse decoration with many types of head ornaments and elaborate curls on hair style. Her attendants are offering a head ornament called chudamandana and other ornaments to be worn. In Figure 13F, the queen is looking into the mirror admiring herself and trying to set right her garment. Her attendant on right side is holding a bangle and the one on left is showing more jewelry for the queen's decoration. One attendant is holding the pet monkey and some fruits for it.

Figure 13H gives a picture of the different names of jewelry used by queens. Some panels show a round decorative ornament on shoulders that was called Baahu valaya (not depicted in Figure 13H) can be seen Figure 14. Figure 13G depicts the head decoration and ornaments of Chalukyan style for a comparative study.

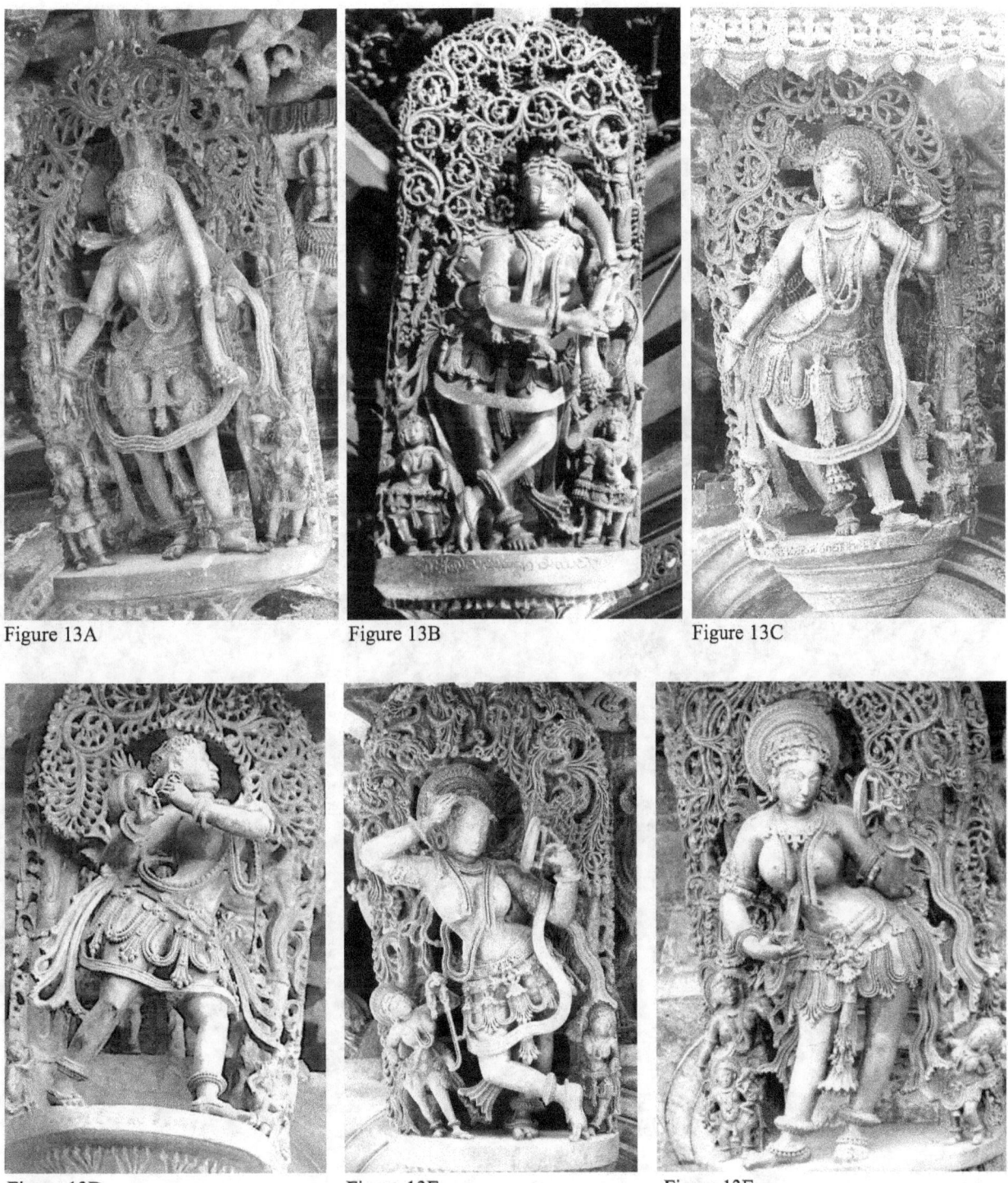

Figure 13A

Figure 13B

Figure 13C

Figure 13D

Figure 13E

Figure 13F

Figure 13A-F: Prema kride - Queens adorning to look their best.

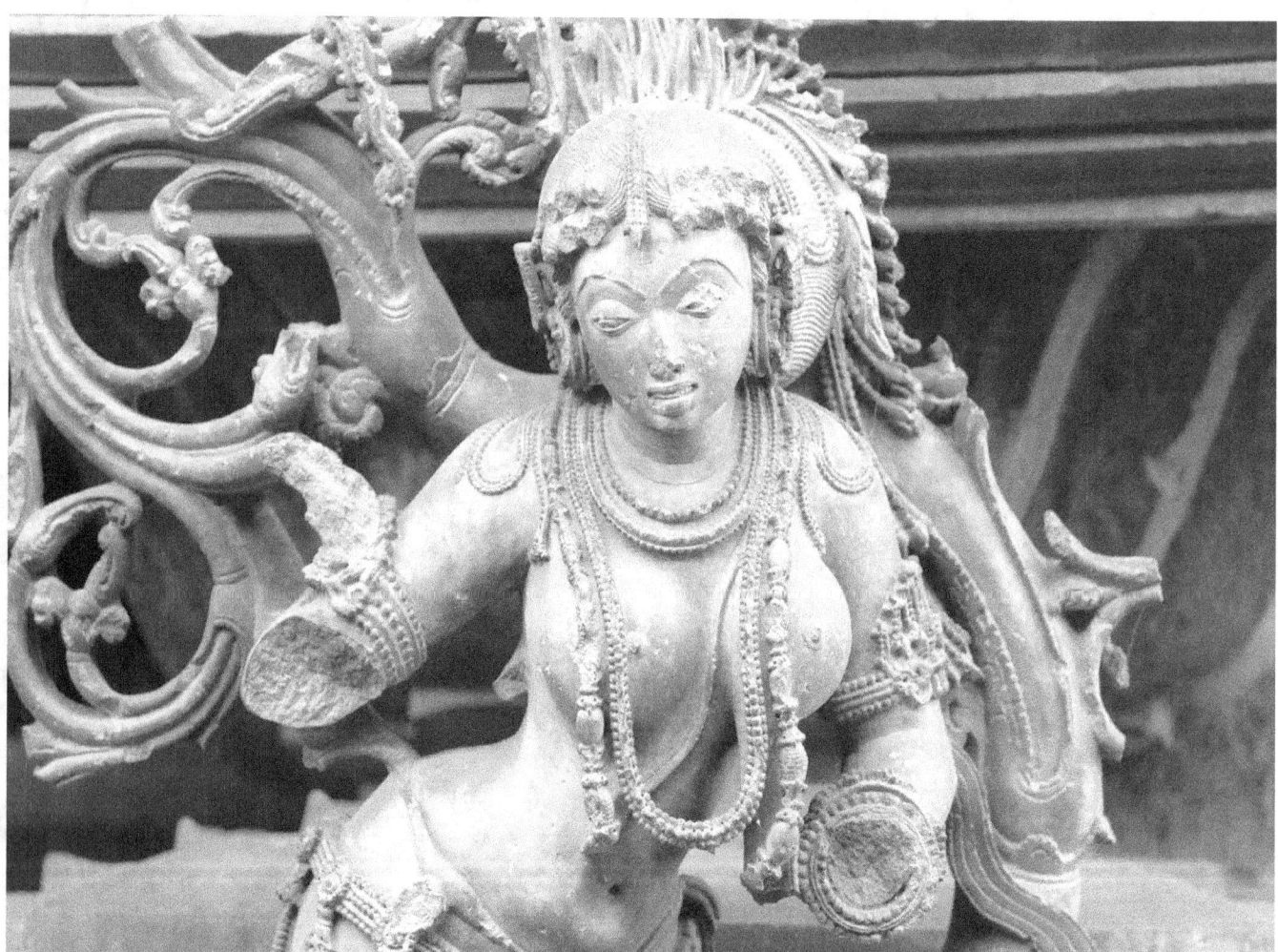

Figure 13G: Shilabalika of Kuruvatti Mallikarjuna temple in Chalukyan style

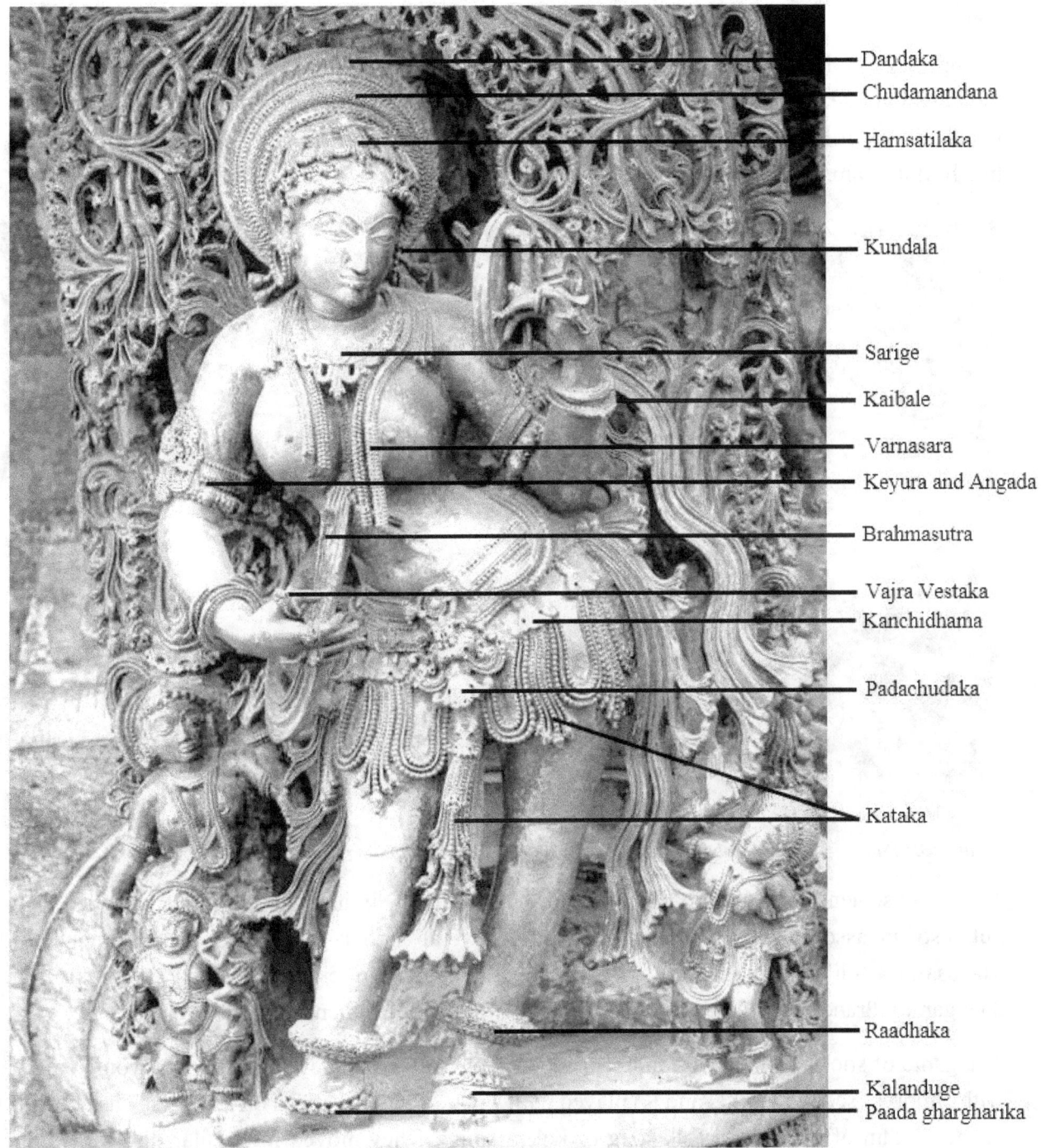

Dandaka
Chudamandana
Hamsatilaka

Kundala

Sarige
Kaibale
Varnasara
Keyura and Angada
Brahmasutra
Vajra Vestaka
Kanchidhama
Padachudaka
Kataka
Raadhaka
Kalanduge
Paada ghargharika

Figure 13H: Identifying the names of the ornaments used by queens in Hoysala style

Other games:

Swing play 'Andolana kride, Shadwala kride' on sand banks were other amusements enjoyed by the king and queens. Besides the organized sports and games, there were number of amusements which the royal families and commoners enjoyed together – They were animal races and fights like buffalo, ram, and cock fights.

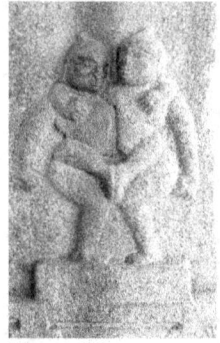
Figure 13I

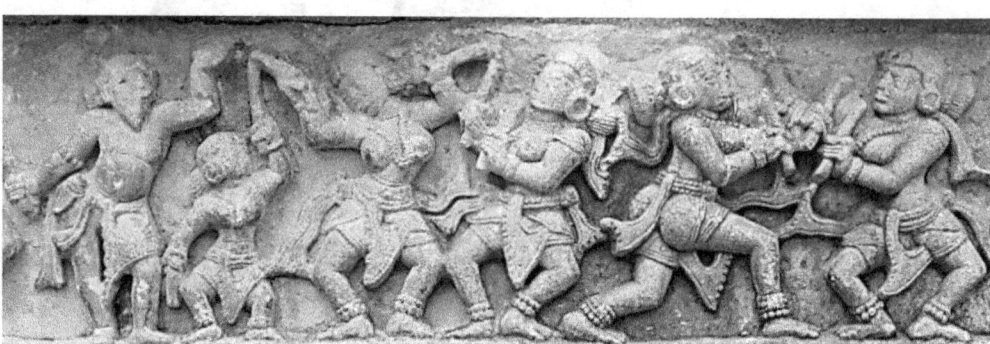
Figure 13J

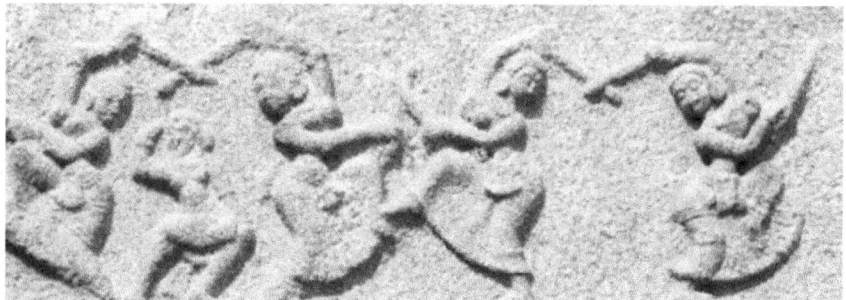
Figure 13K

Figure 13I: Panel depicting acrobatics. Figures 13J and K: Panels depicting Kolata.

These amusements gave them a down to earth joy for happy living and not only a balanced view but also an association with the commoners. Several indoor games are also mentioned in Manasallosa – like Chaturanga, Varatika kride a game of cowries, Phanida or Pashaka krida (a dice game), Prahelika kride – the game of riddles which the women enjoyed in leisure time.

The game of sticks (kolata) was another indoor game of the female folk. Men and women along with children (see figures 13J and K) played with a pair of painted sticks on festivals. They danced to the rhythm of music of a folk song or kolata songs. They moved in circular directions with varieties of footsteps, beating the sticks and creating formations. Many temples have the kolata scenes carved on pillars or on outer walls. On festive occasions men also joined the group for open air performances, accompanied by expert players who delighted the crowd, (Figure 13I) by performing acrobatics- like touching the head with the toes, or mallayuddha the wrestling, and so on.

10.7 Rearing of Pets

Rearing pets was another hobby of royal women. Pigeons, parrots, talking bird myna and monkeys were reared as pets. The sculpture of Belur clearly depicts the berries and grains that were used to feed the pets.

Pigeons were trained to carry letters and messages during Chalukyan period. The male bird was trained to carry letters that was tied round its neck. It would fly from anywhere to the required destination where its home was or the mate was. The letter would be received by the receiving party.

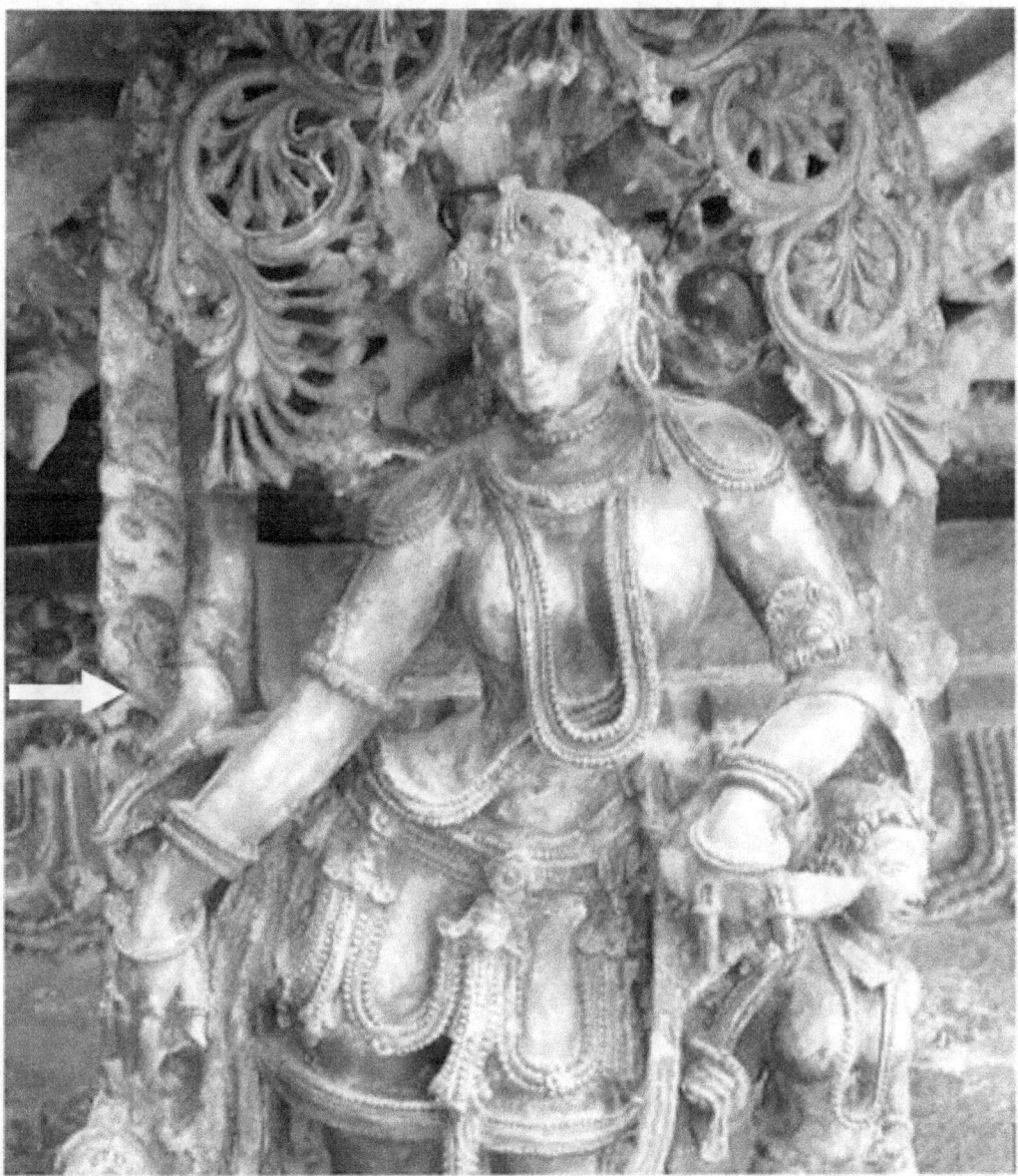

Figure 14: Pet pigeon sitting on the right hand

The fourth vimshati of Manasollasa gives details about what type of pigeon were best suited for rearing as pets. Messenger pigeons are with natural ability to fly back home from any distance as they utilize the earth's geomagnetic field for navigation. They have a built-in map and compass mechanism. Such birds were trained to know and fly to a specific destination and were transported while travelling. The message to be delivered to the queen was tied to it and released as can be seen in the neck of the pigeon and sent as a messenger bird. In Figure 14, the messenger bird is sitting on the right hand of the lady delivering the message. In her left hand is the letter, which was tied to the neck of the pigeon. A young girl, in short tights, is assisting in untying the thread of the message.

Parrot was another favorite pet bird. In Figure 15A, a Lady is seen talking to her pet parrot. Her assistants are holding fruits, berries and grains to pamper the bird. In Figure 15B the lady is seen with another bird, which is playing with her necklace, sitting on her left arm.

Monkeys were also reared as pets of a royal woman. In Fig.13.F, the Lady is decorating herself and her pet monkey is being carried by the short and stout attendant Kaaru who is standing on the right side. In the Figure15.C, the pet monkey is teasing the lady by pulling away her robe and the woman is scaring away the monkey. Queens also had trained deer as a pet dipa mriga(Fig. 15. D) which they used in their hunting expedition. They were trained to respond to the signal call and also indicate about the arrival of wild animals or sober ones when they were taken for hunting games (for details on dipa mriga see ch .10.2 Mrigaya vinoda).

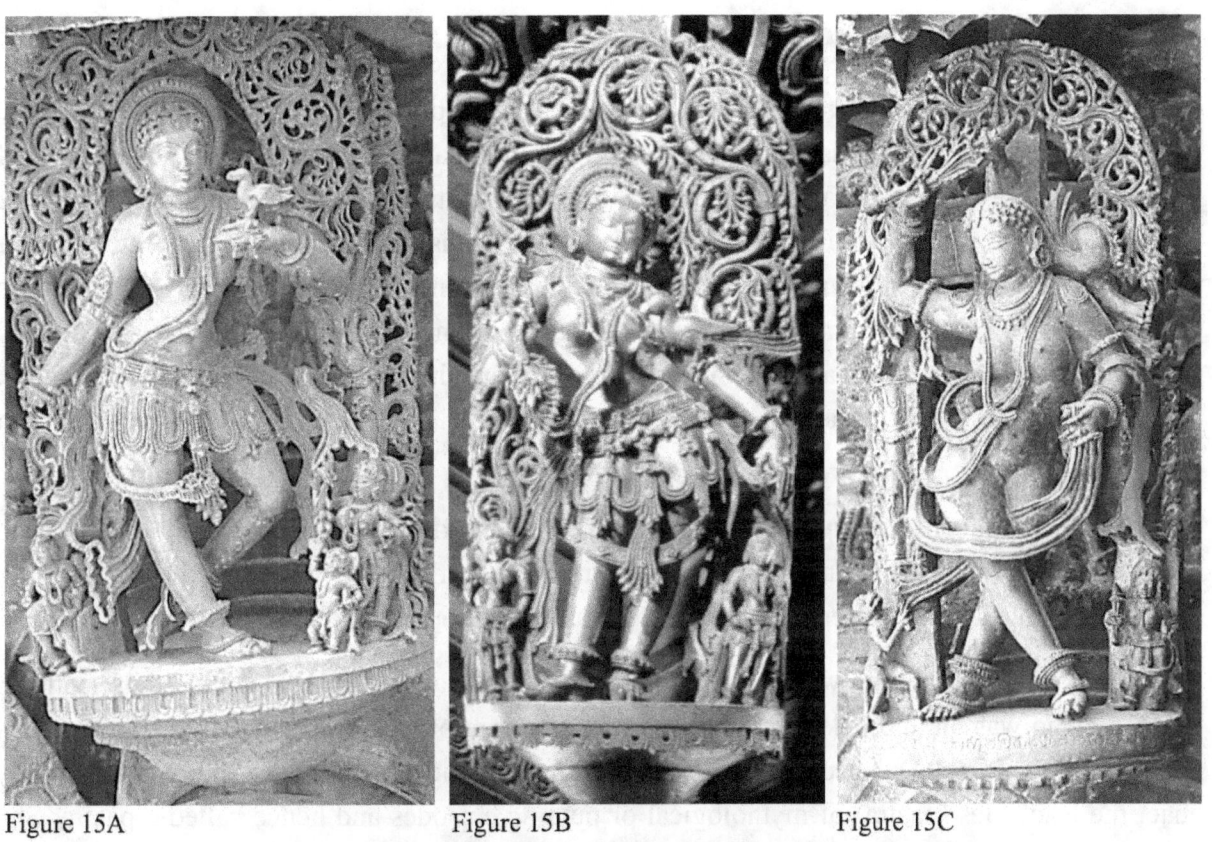

Figure 15A   Figure 15B   Figure 15C

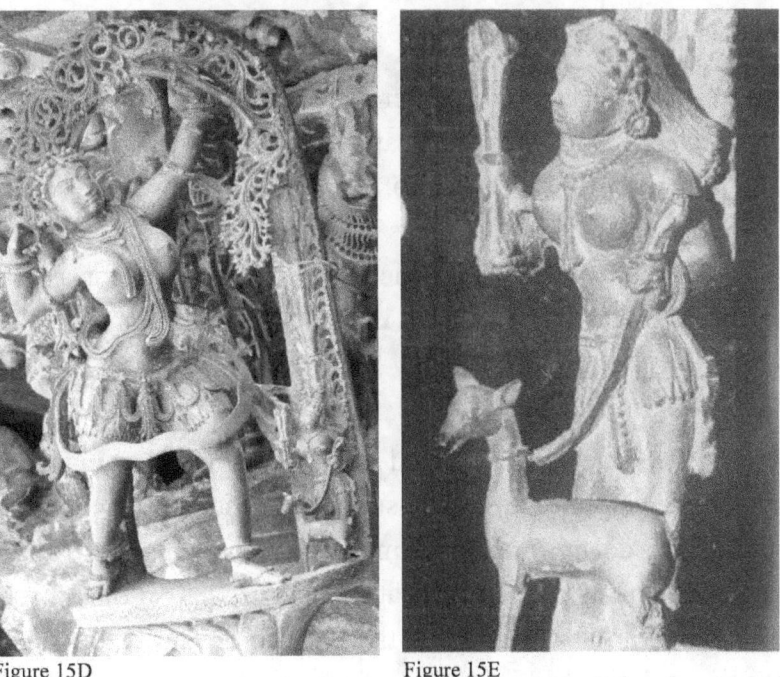

Figure 15D   Figure 15E

Figures 15A-E: Pet animals reared by queens

11. An Insight into the Fine Arts

The fourth vimshati of Manasollasa deals with the many aspects of music and dance under the classification of Vadya vinoda, Nritya vinoda, Gita vinoda and Katha vinoda. In the chapter of vadya vinoda of Manasollasa the four types of instruments-the string, wind, percussion and metallic cymbals (tata, sushira, avanaddha and ghana musical instruments respectively) are discussed. The making of instruments, the varieties of instruments in each group, the techniques of playing the various instruments are also detailed. The rendering of raga in vocal music, and rhythm patterns, the metre (chandas) of presenting songs are also detailed in the book Manasollasa. The various types of string and percussion instruments of Hoysala period are also carved in sculptures.

The inscriptional evidences of Chalukyan and Hoysala period: The inscriptions of temples and Manasollasa has many references regarding the main dancer and the instrumentalists. They are addressed with a slightly different term than Natyashastra though the roles played were similar.

The Nartaki of Natyashastra was called "Paatra" in Chalukyan and Hoysala temple inscriptions. The lady who was the most skilled in both pure dance, interpretative dance, the art of histrionics and music was the prime dancer paatra. She was well trained in arts had the capacity to effectively enact the lead roles (paatra) of mythological or puranic episodes and hence called a paatra. She enjoyed a higher remuneration and a respectable social status as she danced for God in the temple every day.

Nati - The co-dancer of Natyashastra, or another dancer was a Lachhani or Saavagani in temple inscriptions. Lachhani danced along with the paatra with secondary roles. She also appears to be equally well dressed in bracket figures like apsara. Even lachhani was a skilled and well-trained dancer who was well versed in rhythmic patterns of dance and music. Saavagani was a co-singer. She is depicted with metallic cymbals and depicted to be the singer for apsara's dance (Figure 17B) The male singer was Gayaka (Figure 17C) is also depicted in some panels.

11.1 Vadya Vinoda

Sculptures with musical instruments have played a very prominent part in the development of the cultural heritage of India. Sculptures are like visual documentation of various aspects like Love for classical art, musicians, documentation of musical instruments, the method of playing the instruments, and the social status of the artists at that period and so on. Hoysala sculptors have tried to keep a record of the various instruments, that were in use during their period. It mirrors the in-depth knowledge the sculptors had in the use of musical instruments and the intensity of love for dance and music. These panels also reflect the support from patrons, the models who posed, and the interest with which the public supported in the field of arts. Through the apsara sculptures the sculptors have depicted the four main category of instruments like Tata (Figure 16A), Sushira

(Figure 16B), Avanaddha (Figure 16C) and Ghana (Figure 16D) - which were used in a solo or orchestral performance. The depiction of apsara figures playing all four categories of instruments in dancing postures probably suggests that they sequenced the recitals with different instruments alternated by pure dance, expressive dance and literary recitals to break the monotony and ensure variety to retain the public curiosity. It was also the duty of the queen to entertain the king in leisure time.

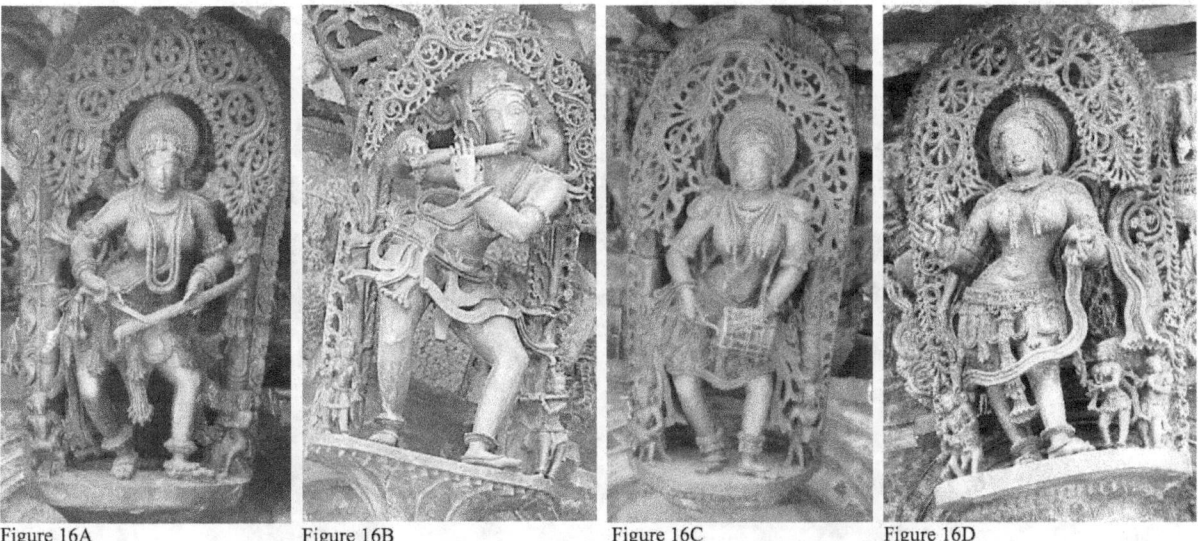

Figure 16A   Figure 16B   Figure 16C   Figure 16D

Figure 16. A-D. Apsaras depicting all four types of instruments- string, wind, percussion and metallic instruments.

The representation of dance in sculptures give a clear picture of the style in which the contemporary dancers performed. The refined dance postures indicate about the refinement that had come about in the art of Hoysala artists, sculptors, promoters, general public.

The Attendants in Vadya Vinoda

Among the other servants of God were the artists who were depicted as dancer, co dancer. Singer and instrumentalists who are in great numbers in the Chalukyan and Hoysala temples, are carved up to knee level, sometimes maddalekaras, playing percussion instruments are in sitting posture as depicted in Figure 17A and 17B. Unlike the other attendants discussed before, the accompanying artists are all in the same height. Vamshiga, the flute player enjoyed the highest remuneration according to inscriptions.

Nartaki is the main dancer and called paatra in Chalukyan inscriptions. Natyasastra – explains in ch.34: stanza 50-54, about the qualities of a "nartaki". A nartaki should be beautiful physically with feminine charm, good qualities, patience, and good manners. She should possess soft and sweet voice, capable of singing in varying notes. She should be an expert in the representation of passion and feelings (hela, and bhava), knowing the representations of sattva (goodness of character), and skilled in the art of acting - abhinaya. She should be skilled in playing the musical instruments, have a knowledge of notes, rhythm and its patterns. She should be clever, capable of using the reasoning power, and above all youthful in age with beauty. A dancer with these qualities and knowing the 64 types of arts, was addressed as a "Nartaki". The apsara figures of Belur are carved with the qualities of a nartaki calling them with the regional name of paatra. Manasollasa calls them as 'Pramodini' (cheerful and pleasure personified) who are eligible to give dance and music recitals. Manasollasa also refers that the pleasant natured king, who was exponent of many arts, well versed in the intricacies of music, dance and literature should be the sabha pati (presiding person).

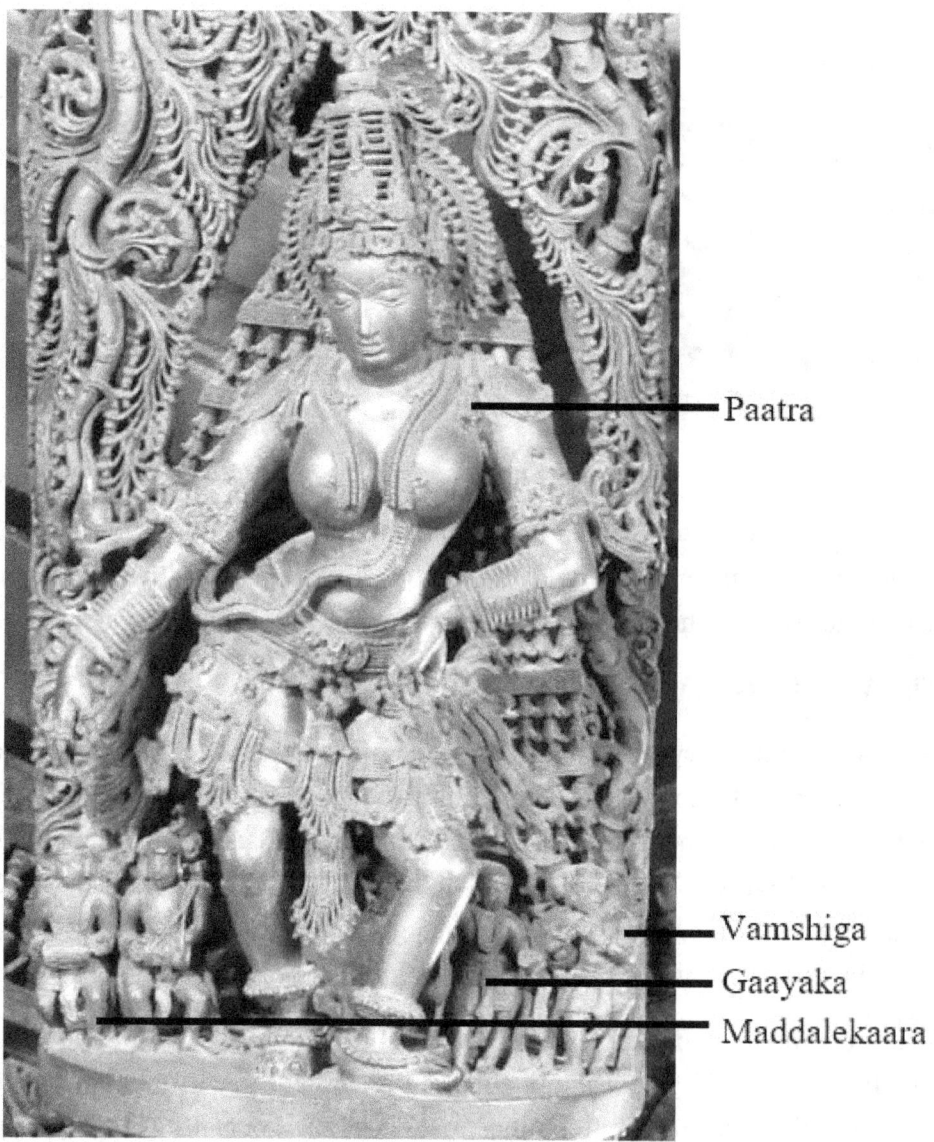

Figure 17A

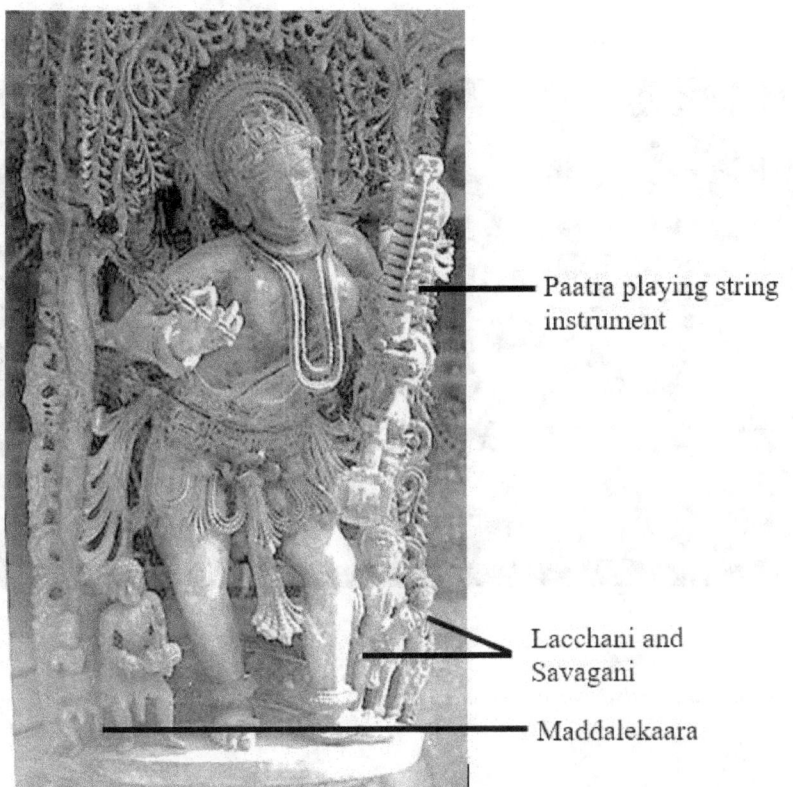

Paatra playing string instrument

Lacchani and Savagani

Maddalekaara

Figure 17B

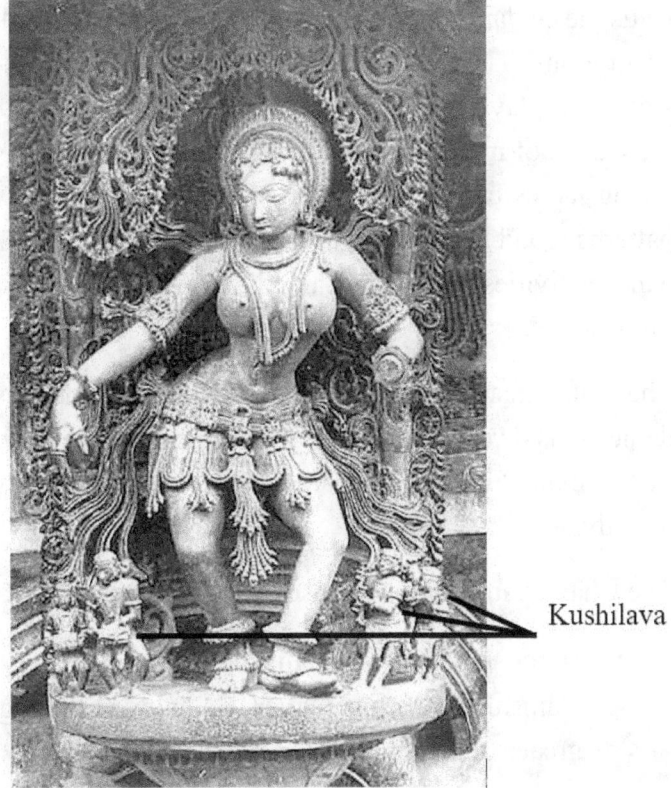

Kushilava

Figure 17C

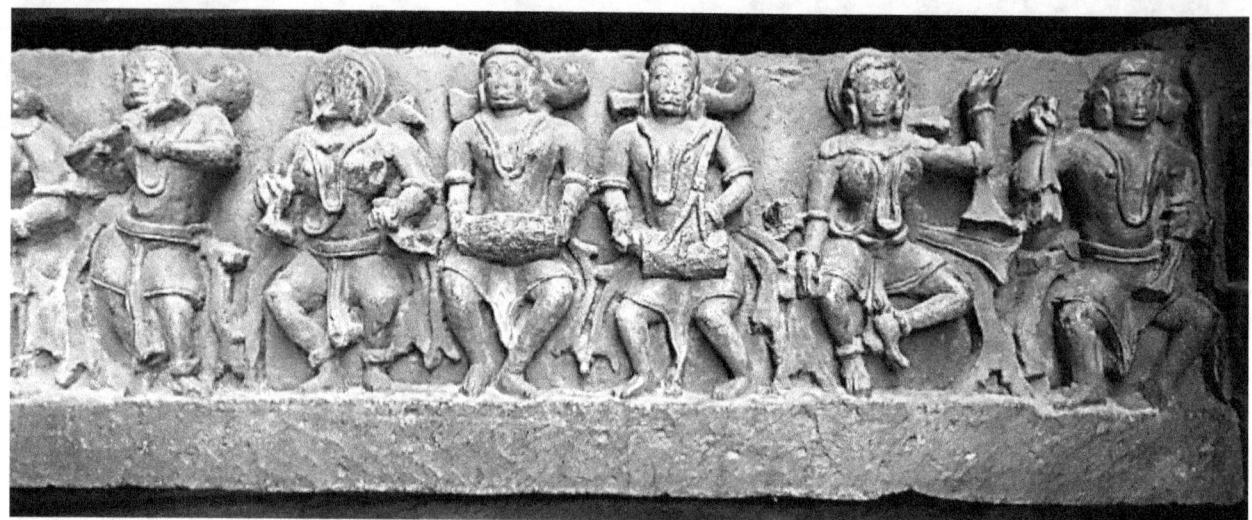

Figure 17D

Figures 17A-C: The male and female accompanying artists Kushilavanu in general terms.

Figure 17C: Kushilava group of instrumentalists

Figure 17D: The panel depicting vamshiga, savagaani, two maddalekaras, nartaki and Natuva in sequence from left to right.

Natis the co dancer appear in height as daasis but are slim and elegant with more jewelry and head decorations. They are present mostly singing with the brass cymbals when the apsara is either singing or playing an instrument or dancing as seen in Fig.17.B and Fig. 19. They are also seen in the panels of musicians (fig. 17.D). Natyashastra (Ch. 34 Stanza.48-49) also refers to a group of young ladies called Natis, who were well versed in music, aware of the intricacies of rhythm patterns, good at abhinaya and well trained in dance. All the apsara images depicting musical or dance activities, are accompanied by Natis, identified later as Savagani or Lachani in the temple inscriptions.

The male artists who are good at playing instruments were in general called Kushilava. They are depicted as dwarf figures along with apsara while dancing, all in the same height, up to the knees of the main Figure. They are playing percussion instruments for rhythm or playing flute for melody.

The Chalukyan inscriptions uses a different term for Kushilava group such as:

- Harekara – Instrumentalist
- Vamshiga - A flute player. He enjoyed the highest status in the group of musicians with greater remuneration.

54

- Maddalekaara - A Percussionist. Maddalekaaras were two in number. The first and the second one. Every apsara Figure depicting her music or dance recitals is seen with two maddalekaaras. The two types of percussion instruments were with the intention of special effects while dancing, breaking the monotony as it was played continuously during a dance recital. The maddalekaras also indicate the rhythm based pure dance aspect of dance. Many panels of lord Shiva dancing also show two maddalekaras which indicated the rhythm aspect in Shiva's dance.
- Gaayaka - A Singer, could also be the teacher Natuva who sings or plays cymbals.

In every recital of apsara all the above-mentioned artists participated. Natis and Kushilava are present as dwarf attendants giving music in all the apsara sculptures, that are engaged in activities of dance or music, as narrated in Venisamhaara (a Sanskrit drama by Bhasa who dates prior to Kalidaasa, 4th century approximately) as Tatkimiti Naarambhayasi Kushilavaih Saha Sangitakam - Meaning the Lady presented music along with the Kushilavaih.

11.2 Nritya Vinoda

The fifth vimshati of Manasollasa and Abhinaya Darpana explains the three types of dance as Nritta, Nritya and Natya along with a detailed account of various intricacies involved in the art of dance.

1. Nritta - pure dance, a form of dance devoid of sentiments or Rasa and psychological states. The panels depict limbs of the dancer in symmetrical form and rhythmic movements guided only by percussion instruments can be analysed to be showing Nritta aspect (Figure 18A). It is performed in religious occasion like procession of the image of deity, coronation, marriage or birth of a son and so on.

2. Nritya - interpretative rhythmic dance where rhythm and lyrical elements preponderate. It is a combination of rhythmic movements along with psychological states of bhava and sentiments of the song performed mostly in king's court (Figure 18B). The percussionist and singer play the music. The words and sentiment of the song are conveyed through abhinaya by the dancer.

3. Natya - a recital with some elements of drama / Naataka, a lyrico dramatical presentation which has some traditional story called rupaka in Sanskrit along with minor part of rhythmic and interpretative aspects. (Figure 18C and 18D). It involves the use of suitable accessories in hand and settings on stage.

The gesticulations of hand and body movements are all depicted in detail as interpreted in Natya shastra are also seen in Manasollasa. One can observe all these aspects in the bracket figures which shows pure dance being supported only by percussion instruments. The interpretative dance by a combination of percussion instrument, melody instrument like flute and the words of the songs rendered by singing dwarf figures. When vocal singing, instrument and dance are combined it is called "Turya tritaya" in Manasollasa. Natya which involves dramatic representations along with gesticulations and use of accessories in hands or through dress to dramatize a scene are all indicated in the group of sculptures depicting dance. Though many panels have accessories in hand, the dance related ones are with accompanying instruments.

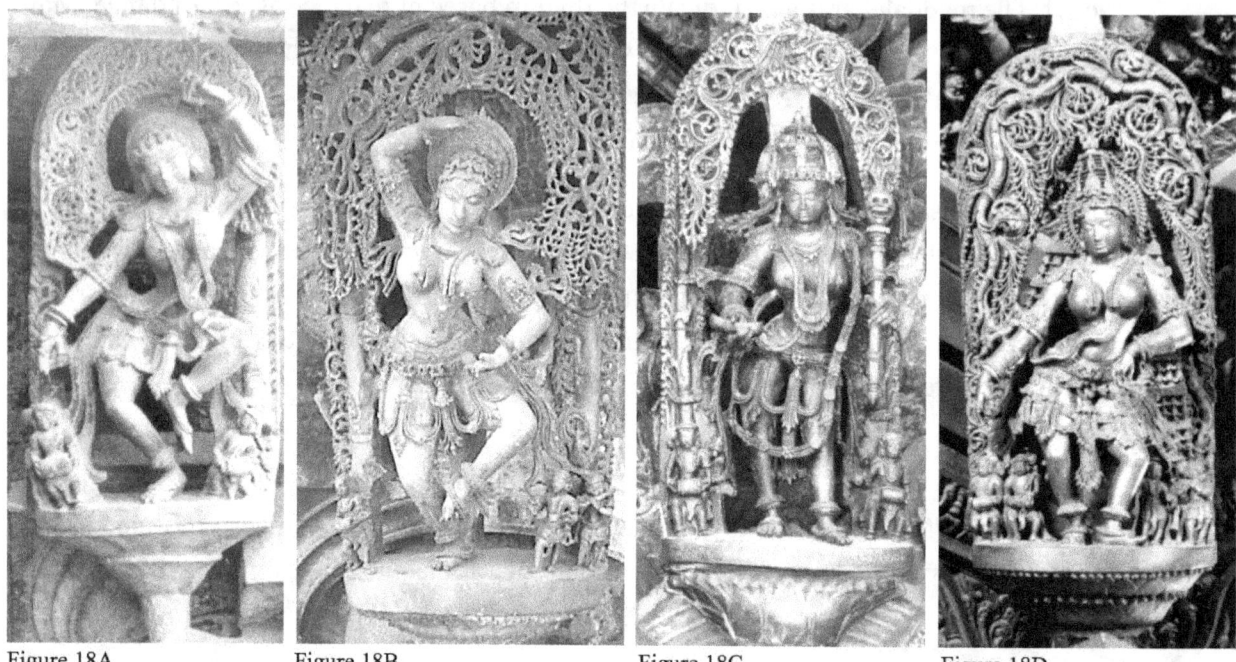

Figure 18A   Figure 18B   Figure 18C   Figure 18D

Figure 18A-D: Depiction of depiction of Nritta, Nritya and Natya identifiable by the depiction of instrumentalists.

Music, dance, drama, discussions and debates formed an integral part of intellectual preoccupation. The queens of Chalukyan and Hoysala dynasties were great lovers of art and were well trained in instrumental music, percussion instruments, singing and dancing. Around 450 slokas, from 950 – 1400, is a discussion on the intricacies involved with dance. Many panels indicate that the queens were musicians, dancers and well versed in playing varieties of instruments. They entertained the king with their skills in the divine art. The dancers were trained to play and dance carrying the stringed and percussion instruments.

11.3 Gita Vinoda

Gita vinoda is a very elaborate chapter in the 4th vimshati of Manasollasa that has descriptions of where the king as sabhapati should be seated and who else should be present for the gita recital. The qualities of the singer are in detail for how proficient should the singer be in various ragas, rhythm, melody aspects, language and the knowledge of metres in which the song is composed. The king who was also well informed about the related texts would discuss about the swara, raaga and taala renditions and also sing and demonstrate some unique aspects. In the Figure 19A, the queen or the paatra is beating the cup shaped brass cymbals and engrossed in singing. The co singer savagani is also with cymbals which indicates about the importance of rhythm in singing. The main singer gives the beat and movements which is followed by the co singer. Three types of instruments like flute, percussion and metallic instrument can be seen by the kushilava group.

Manasollasa fourth vimshati mentions a different type of playing the percussion instrument called 'Charyagaana'. Charya means movement. When the instrument is played along with jumping or turning movements it is charyagaana (see Figure 19B). The percussion instrument is hour glass shaped with the central part as narrow as can be held in the fist. The central part is tied by the rope which the player wears. The stick or Kona is used to rub the right part of the instrument.

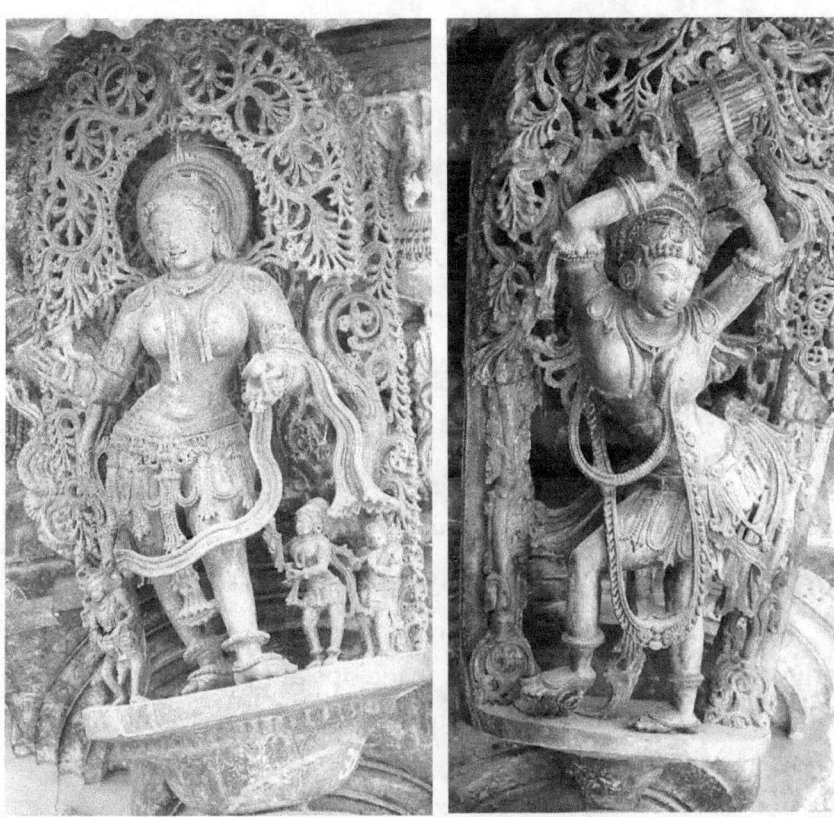

Figure 19A   Figure 19B

Figure 19A: Queen / Apsara engrossed in singing, Gita Vinoda. Figure 19B: In charya gaana.

11.4 Katha Vinoda

Another sculpture Fig. 20.A, depicts a queen going through a discussion, or narrating an episode from the scriptures. Katha vinoda was another pastime of the kings Manasollasa mentions that Chalukyan queens were good debaters and took part in discussion sessions. The king used to listen to heroic stories and puranic episodes narrated by his own queens in privacy. Manasollasa says that the king and the members of the harem were well versed in Natyashastra and puranic episodes. They were good at enacting dramatic situations. The king enjoyed the recitation of mythological and puranic episodes through "katha vinoda". It was "Dvivaktra" where two people rendered it as a dialogue, or called chaturmukha, when it was a group rendering.

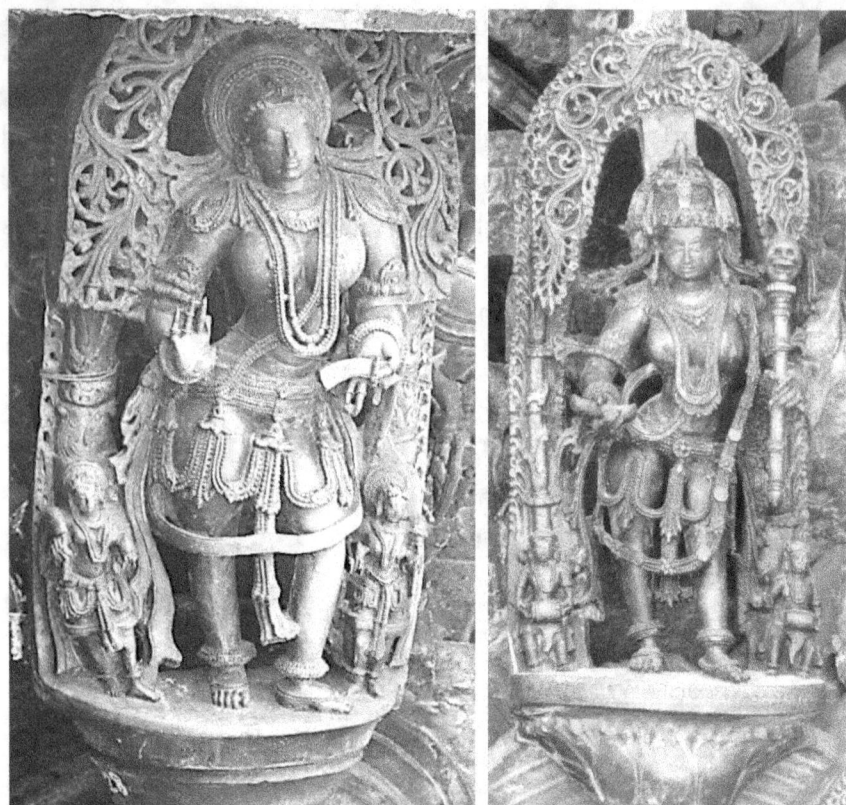

Figure 20A   Figure 20B

Figure 20A: Queen going through a discussion. Figure 20B: Queen decorated like Bahiravi

A lady is seen here in Figure 20B, decorated like a 'Bhairavi' and enacting a related episode. The maddalekaras on either side are supporting the for the vigorous gait which the main figure is depicting. She also has accessories like khatwanga (a weapon made of skull and bone or staff) in hand and skull studded crown the use of which are discussed in the 'Aharya" chapter of Natyashastra.

The panels depicting dance and music indicates the cultural aspects of Hoysala period. One can study the types of string and percussion instruments used, the types of footsteps performed in dance, the accessories used in dramatic representations and also the usage of various ornaments. All the details regarding the social life of royal families are depicted in a very interesting way in Manasollasa.

12. Conclusion

Manasollasa is a great source of information to study the social life of royal families of Chalukya and Hoysala dynasties. The activities of royal women and their enthusiasm for arts and sports are described beautifully in the 4th and 5th parts of Manasollasa. An artistic representation of such happy moments is carved in stone in both the Chalukyan and Hoysala temples. The glory of queens, their refinement in personality, love for adventure, animals, nature, and fine arts are all beautifully projected in the bracket figures of apsara sculptures of Belur Chennakeshava temple. The panels with similar themes are not fixed in a series or order. Reasons for this are not clear. However, when the pictures with same activity were arranged, the theme continuation could be traced according to how it is described in Manasollasa.

The intricacies involved in both the dancing figures and the figures handling instruments revealed that the style was as described in Natyashastra which was common all over India. The dance of apsaras is therefore cannot be compared to any one style of the present-day regional styles that shaped up in post medieval period and presented as classical styles of Indian dancing in the present period. A comparative study of Manasollasa and the sculptural panels recreates the world of Hoysala queens.

It is interesting to note that even today, the classical styles of Indian dance forms are presented along with the accompaniment of nattuva, gaayaka, savagani, maddalekara, and vamshiga. These are also depicted in the shilabalika panels. This suggests that the paatra of Chalukya and Hoysala period are in the classical style of dance as described in Natyashastra. This cultural heritage is a continuum that originates from the initial days of Natyashastra. However, Natyashastra does not address aspects of the social life of kings and queens. This particular aspect is covered in Manasollasa. Manasollasa also goes by the rules laid out in Natyashastra and hence should be considered as a primary text to analyze the sculptures of Chalukyan or Hoysala temples.

13. Bibliography

Photo credits:

My sincere thanks to the following for allowing me to use their photographs for this book:
- Amar Reddy, from Pune for the pictures of Shilabalikas
- Professor Gianluigi Vezoli.
- Muralikrishna Maddikeri from Bellary, A History and heritage enthusiast.
- Nataraj K.V. Dudhihalli, Davanagere
- American Institute of Indian Studies, Gurgaon.
- Thrilling Travels Blog by Ami Bhat: https://thrillingtravel.in/
- Cover page image by Dr. Rohitha Eswer, Mysore.

Books and Articles Referred:

- Apsaras in Hoysala art - A new dimension, By Rekha Rao, Published by Aryan Books International, 2009, ISBN- 978-81-7305-379-5
- Kalyana Chakukya Devalayagalu Ondu Samskrutika Adhyayana", H.S.Gopal Rao,1993).
- Manasollasa, edited by Dr. M.M. Kalaburgi, volume 1 and 2 – A publication of Prasaranga, - Karnatak university, Dharvad, 1998.
- Manasollasa, Vol. 1, G. K. Shri Gondekar O.R.I. Baroda, 1925
- Somesvara's Manasollasa; A cultural study. By Shiv shekhar Mishra
- Indian Temple Architecture; Form and Transformation, By Adam Hardy. Published by Indira Gandhi National Centre for the Arts.
- Hoysala Dynasty – Editor Sheikh Ali. Publication - Prasaranga University of Mysore, Mysore. Year – 1972. With special reference to article - by Settar S. Salabhanjikas with special reference to Belur.
- Encyclopedia of Indian Temple Architecture - South India Upper Dravida Desha - Later Phase. Published by American Institute of Indian Studies.
- Hoysala Temples by S. Settar Vol. 2.
- The Hoysala Artists: Their Identity and Styles. By Kelleson Collyer. Published by Directorate of Archeology and Museums, Mysore.
- A guide to Belur Chennakeshava Temple. By L. Narasimhachar. Directorate of Archeology and museums, Government of Karnataka.
- Studies in Natyasastra: With special reference to the Sanskrit drama in performance. By G. H. Tarlekar. Motilal Banarsidass Publishers Pvt. Ltd., Delhi.
- Natyasastra (Kannada). By Prof. Adya Rangacharya. Published by Akshara Prakashana, Sagar, Karnataka (577401). For Ninasam Theatre Institute, Heggodu.
- Dasharoopaka (Kannada): Translation of the Sanskrit treatise on dramaturgy by Dhananjaya and commentary by Dhanika (both 10 century AD) with detailed introduction and notes. By K. V. Subbanna, Published by Ninasam Theatre Institute, Akshara Prakashana, Heggodu, 1992.
- Nandikesvara Abhinaya Darpanam: A manual of gesture and posture used in ancient Indian dance and drama. By Dr. Manmohan Ghosh. Published by Moni Sanyal for the Manisha Granthalaya Pvt. Ltd., 4/36 Bankin Chatterjee Street, Calcutta – 12, 1992.
- The Natyasastra – Vol 1 and 2. Edited by Dr. Manmohan Ghosh, 1995, Calcutta.
- Vadya Darshan: An exhibition of Indian musical instruments. Lalitkala Galleries, Ravindra Bhavan, New Delhi. Sangeet Natak Academy, National Academy of Music, Dance and Drama, New Delhi.
- Bharata's Art: Then and Now. By Dr. Padma Subramanyan.
- The Mysticism of Music, Sound and Word. By Hazrat Inayat Khan, The Sufi message Vol. II.
- Web site "Social life in medieval Karnataka" by Jyotsna K. Kamath.
  https://commons.wikimedia.org/wiki/File:Hoysaleswara_Sculpture_3,_Halebidu.jpg

About the Author

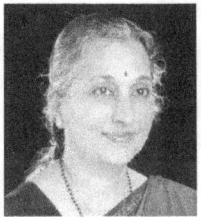 Rekha Rao, a master's degree holder in Indology from University of Mysore, is also an accomplished classical dancer. In the year 2000, she took up independent research work in Indology under the guidance of Dr. S.R.Rao, Former Deputy Director General, Archaeological survey of India, and since 2010, on her own. Her interests in the temple sculptures have made her visit and study various temples in India focusing on the sculptures of Apsaras, Buddhist architecture and Indus Seals.

Books by the same Author

Amazon.com author page: www.amazon.com/author/rekharao

1. Yoga in Indian Temple Sculptures: A New Perspective, Available online on Amazon in both eBook and print book format:
https://www.amazon.in/Yoga-Indian-Temple-Sculptures-Perspective-ebook/dp/B076FVZFLR/ref=asap_bc?ie=UTF8

2. Erotic Sculptures in Indian Temples: A New Perspective, Available online on Amazon in both eBook and Print Format:
https://www.amazon.in/Erotic-Sculptures-Indian-Temples-Perspective-ebook/dp/B076J1TNT7/ref=asap_bc?ie=UTF8

3. Symbolography in Indus seals, Available online on Amazon in both eBook and Print Format:
https://www.amazon.in/Symbolography-Indus-Seals-Rekha-Rao-ebook/dp/B016QQKBQE

4. Buddhism in Rani Ki Vav, Patan - A World Heritage Monument, Sold by Amazon Digital Services, Inc, ASIN: B00Y6UXHPK. Available online on Amazon: http://amzn.to/2dGc9WG

5. Rani Ki Vav – The Abode of Bodhisattva and Dakinis, Published by Aditya Prakashan, New Delhi, 2014, ISBN: 9788177421354

6. Vajrayana Buddhism in Khajuraho Sculptures, Published by Power Publishers, 2012, ISBN – 978-93-82070-02-3, ISBN – 93-82070-02-3

7. Science and Golden Ratios in Mandala Architecture, Published by D.K Printworld (P) Ltd., 2011, ISBN – 81-246-0587-4, ISBN – 978-81-246-0587-5

8. Apsaras in Hoysala art - A new dimension, Published by Aryan Books International, 2009, ISBN- 978-81-7305-379-5

9. Therapeutics in Indian sculptures - Ranki vav, Patan, Published by Aryan books international, 2006, 2007, ISBN – 81-7305-312-x, ISBN – 9788173053122

10. The Depiction of Vedic Priests in Indus Seals, Available online on Amazon in both ebook and print book format:
https://www.amazon.com/Depiction-Vedic-Priests-Indus-Seals/dp/1717855202/ref=sr_1_9?ie=UTF8&qid=1537762482&sr=8-9&keywords=Rekha+rao

11. The Dictionary of Indus Symbols, Available online on Amazon in both ebook and print book format:
https://www.amazon.com/gp/product/1726820335/ref=dbs_a_def_rwt_bibl_vppi_i0

www.ingramcontent.com/pod-product-compliance
Lightning Source LLC
Chambersburg PA
CBHW080835170526
45158CB00009B/2567